I0088415

AUTOMATIC RIFLE
(BROWNING)

MODEL OF 1918

SERVICE HANDBOOK

PREPARED IN THE OFFICE OF
THE CHIEF OF ORDNANCE

REVISED
March, 1921

WASHINGTON
GOVERNMENT PRINTING OFFICE
1921

Published by Books Express Publishing
Copyright © Books Express, 2011
ISBN 978-1-78039-508-1

Books Express publications are available from all good retail and online booksellers. For
publishing proposals and direct ordering please contact us at: info@books-express.com

WAR DEPARTMENT,

WASHINGTON, *January 26, 1920.*

The following pamphlet, entitled "Automatic Rifle (Browning), Model of 1918, Service Handbook" (revised), which supersedes War Department Document No. 853 and all other publications on the same subject issued prior to this date, is published for the information and guidance of all concerned.

[062.11, A. G. O.]

BY ORDER OF THE SECRETARY OF WAR:

PEYTON C. MARCH,
General, Chief of Staff.

OFFICIAL:

P. C. HARRIS,
The Adjutant General.

3

TABLE OF CONTENTS.

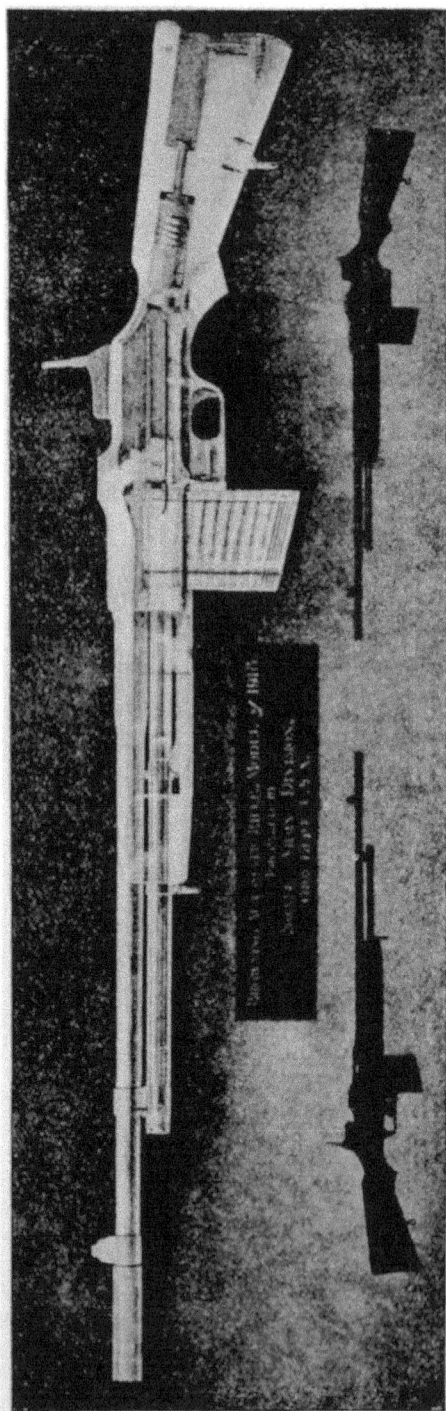

AUTOMATIC RIFLE (BROWNING).

(MODEL OF 1918.)

GENERAL INFORMATION.

GENERAL DESCRIPTION AND DATA.

1. The Browning automatic rifle, model of 1918, is air cooled, gas operated, and magazine fed. It is chambered for U. S. caliber .30, model 1906, ammunition.

2. It has no special cooling system, the barrel being exposed to the air, and the hand of the firer being protected on the under side of the barrel by a large wooden forearm. Care must be taken to avoid touching the barrel during firing.

3. The Browning automatic rifle is operated by the power furnished by expanding powder gases following ignition of the cartridge. These powder gases expand through a port in the barrel and act upon the head of a piston, driving it to the rear. During rearward movement the processes of unlocking, extraction, ejection, and compression of the recoil spring are effected; during the forward movement, feeding, locking, and igniting the cartridges are accomplished.

4. The rifle is fed from a magazine having a capacity of 20 cartridges.

5. This rifle can be fired effectively from all positions prescribed in the Small Arms Firing Manual. It is capable of being fired at the rate of 150 rounds per minute, semiautomatic. The rate of fire, however, which gives the best results in the normal case is 40 to 60 shots per minute, semiautomatic.

6. Right and left side of gun.

1. Weight of rifle, 15 pounds 8 ounces.
2. Weight of magazine, empty, 7 ounces.
3. Weight of magazine, filled, 1 pound 7 ounces.
4. Length of barrel, 24 inches.
5. Over-all length, 47 inches.
6. Sights graduated to 1,600 yards.
7. Caliber bore, 0.30 inch.
8. Gas port from muzzle. 6 inches.
9. Rate of uninterrupted automatic fire (cyclic rate), 600 shots per minute.
10. Chamber pressure, 47,000 to 50,000 pounds per square inch.
11. Muzzle velocity, about 2,680 feet per second.
12. Habitual type of fire, semiautomatic.
13. Head space limits, 1.937 inches to 1.943 inches.
14. Length recoil spring, 15.5 inches.

NOMENCLATURE

7. Numerical (Plates I, II, III) :

1. Receiver.
2. Top plate.
3. Bolt support, right.
4. Bolt support, left.
5. Bolt support rivet.
10. Trigger guard.
11. Trigger guard retaining pin.
12. Trigger guard retaining pin handle.
13. Trigger.
14. Trigger pin (same as 35).
15. Connector pin.
16. Connector.
17. Change lever.
18. Change lever spring.
19. Sear stop.
20. Change lever stop.
21. Change lever stop spring.
22. Change lever stop spring pin.
23. Sear.
24. Sear pin.
25. Sear carrier.
26. Sear spring.
27. Connector stop.
28. Counter-recoil spring.
29. Ejector.
30. Ejector lock.
31. Ejector lock spring.
32. Magazine catch.
33. Magazine catch spring.
34. Magazine release.
35. Magazine catch pin (same as 14).
40. Recoil spring.
41. Recoil spring guide.
42. Recoil spring guide head.
45. Slide.
46. Gas piston.
47. Gas piston bushing.
48. Gas piston plug.
49. Gas piston retaining pin.
50. Gas cylinder.
51. Gas cylinder lock.
52. Gas cylinder tube.
53. Gas cylinder tube retaining pin.
54. Gas cylinder tube retaining pin handle.
55. Gas cylinder tube retaining pin key.
56. Gas cylinder tube bracket.
57. Gas cylinder tube bracket pin.

60. Barrel.
61. Front sight carrier.
62. Front sight carrier key.
63. Front sight carrier key pin.
64. Front sight blade.
65. Buffer tube.
66. Buffer.
67. Buffer friction cone (4).
68. Buffer friction cup (4).
69. Buffer nut.
70. Buffer spring.
72. Bolt guide.
73. Bolt guide spring.
75. Bolt.
76. Firing pin.
77. Extractor.
78. Extractor spring.
80. Bolt lock.
81. Bolt lock pin.
82. Link.
83. Link pin.
85. Hammer.
86. Hammer pin.
88. Operating handle.
89. Operating handle plunger.
90. Operating handle plunger pin.
91. Operating handle plunger spring.
94. Rear sight base.
95. Rear sight spring.
96. Rear sight spring screw.
97. Rear sight axis screw.
98. Rear sight axis screw nut.
99. Rear sight slide.
100. Rear sight slide catch.
101. Rear sight slide catch spring.
102. Rear sight slide stop screw.
103. Rear sight slide catch axis pin.
104. Rear sight leaf.
108. Magazine tube.
109. Magazine base.
110. Magazine follower.
111. Magazine spring.
114. Magazine filler.
115. Combination tool.
118. Forearm (wood).
119. Forearm screw (short).
120. Forearm screw (long).
121. Forearm escutcheon.
125. Butt stock.
126. Butt stock bolt.

PLATE I

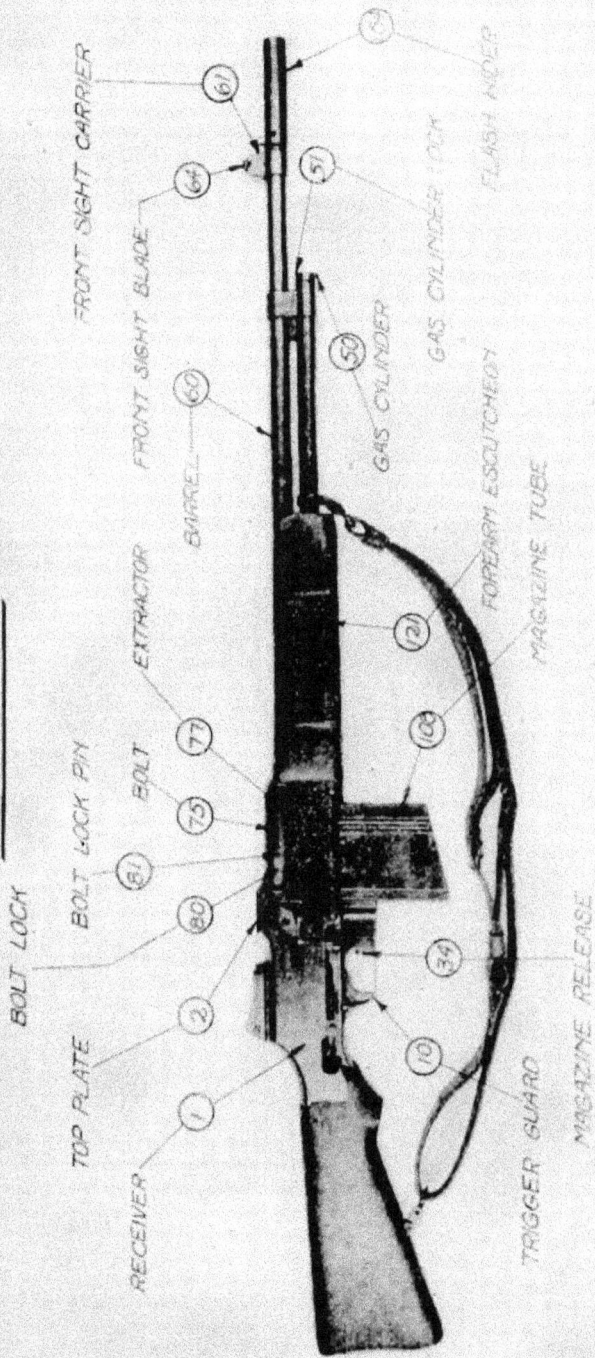

BOLT LOCK

BOLT LOCK PIN

TOP PLATE

BOLT

EXTRACTOR

RECEIVER

BARREL

FRONT SIGHT BLADE

FRONT SIGHT CARRIER

GAS CYLINDER

GAS CYLINDER LOCK

FLASH HIDER

FOREARM ESCUTCHEON

MAGAZINE TUBE

TRIGGER GUARD

MAGAZINE RELEASE

SECTIONALIZED

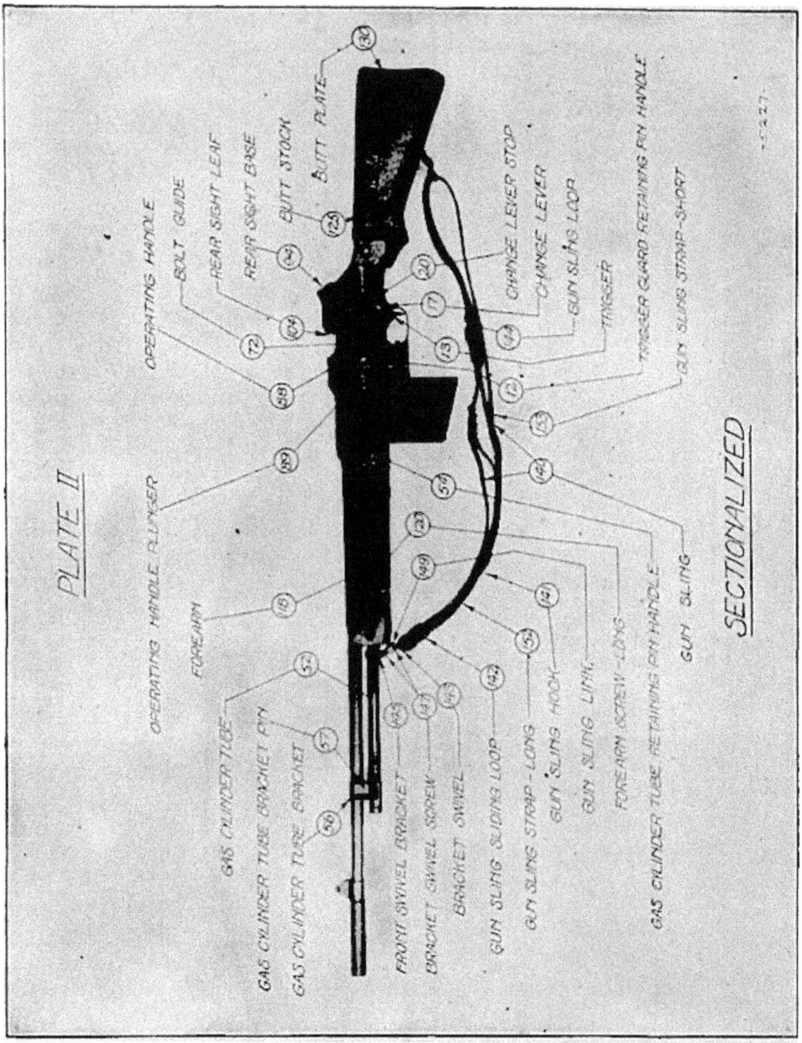

PLATE II

SECTIONALIZED

OPERATING HANDLE PLUNGER
OPERATING HANDLE
BOLT GUIDE
REAR SIGHT LEAF
REAR SIGHT BASE
BUTT STOCK
BUTT PLATE
CHANGE LEVER STOP
CHANGE LEVER
GUN SLING LOOP
TRIGGER
TRIGGER GUARD RETAINING PIN HANDLE
GUN SLING STRAP-SHORT
GUN SLING
GAS CYLINDER TUBE RETAINING PIN HANDLE
FOREARM SCREW-LONG
GUN SLING LINK
GUN SLING HOOK
GUN SLING STRAP-LONG
GUN SLING SLIDING LOOP
BRACKET SWIVEL
BRACKET SWIVEL SCREW
FRONT SWIVEL BRACKET
GAS CYLINDER TUBE BRACKET
GAS CYLINDER TUBE BRACKET PIN
GAS CYLINDER TUBE
FOREARM

10

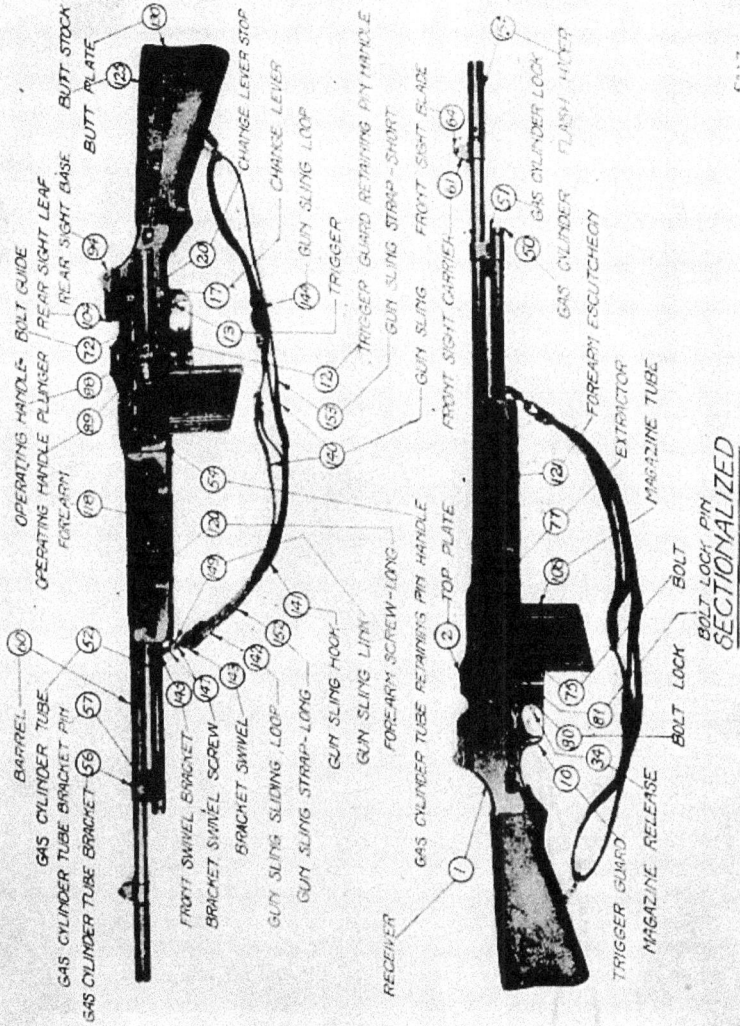

PLATE III

SECTIONALIZED

11

127. Butt stock bolt washer.
130. Butt plate.
131. Butt plate trap.
132. Butt plate trap spring.
133. Butt plate trap axis pin.
134. Butt plate trap spring screw.
136. Butt plate screw (long).
137. Butt plate screw (short).
140. Gun sling (complete).
141. Gun sling hook (3).
142. Gun sling sliding loop.
143. Bracket swivel (2).

144. Gun sling loop.
145. Front swivel bracket.
146. Gun sling hook rivets (9).
147. Bracket swivel screw (4).
148. Gun sling swivel (2).
149. Gun swivel link (2).
150. Butt swivel bracket.
151. Butt swivel bracket screw (2).
152. Gun sling strap (long) .
153. Gun sling strap (short).
154. Flash hider.

8. Alphabetical:

60. Barrel.
75. Bolt.
72. Bolt guide.
73. Bolt guide spring.
80. Bolt lock.
81. Bolt lock pin.
4. Bolt support, left.
3. Bolt support, right.
5. Bolt support rivet.
143. Bracket swivel (2).
147. Bracket swivel screw (4).
66. Buffer.
67. Buffer friction cone (4).
68. Buffer friction cup (4).
69. Buffer nut.
70. Buffer spring.
65. Buffer tube.
130. Butt plate.
136. Butt plate screw (long).
137. Butt plate screw (short).
131. Butt plate trap.
133. Butt plate trap axis pin.
132. Butt plate trap spring.
134. Butt plate trap spring screw.
125. Butt stock.
126. Butt stock bolt.
127. Butt stock bolt washer.
150. Butt swivel bracket.
151. Butt swivel bracket screw.
17. Change lever.
18. Change lever spring.
20. Change lever stop.
21. Change lever stop spring.
22. Change lever stop spring pin.
115. Combination tool.
16. Connector.
15. Connector pin.
27. Connector stop.
28. Counter-recoil spring.
29. Ejector.

30. Ejector lock.
31. Ejector lock spring.
77. Extractor.
78. Extractor spring.
76. Firing pin.
154. Flash hider.
118. Forearm (wood).
121. Forearm escutcheon.
120. Forearm screw (long).
119. Forearm screw (short).
64. Front sight blade.
63. Front sight carrier key pin.
61. Front sight carrier.
62. Front sight carrier key.
145. Front swivel bracket.
50. Gas cylinder.
51. Gas cylinder lock.
52. Gas cylinder tube.
56. Gas cylinder tube bracket.
57. Gas cylinder tube bracket pin.
53. Gas cylinder tube retaining pin.
54. Gas cylinder tube re-
    taining pin handle.   } Assembled.
55. Gas cylinder tube re-
    taining pin key.
46. Gas piston.
47. Gas piston bushing.
48. Gas piston plug.
49. Gas piston retaining pin.
140. Gun sling (complete).
141. Gun sling hook (3).
142. Gun sling sliding loop.
144. Gun sling loop.
146. Gun sling hook rivets (9).
148. Gun sling swivel (2).
149. Gun sling link (2).
152. Gun sling strap (long).
153. Gun sling strap (short). .
85. Hammer.
86. Hammer pin.

PLATE IV.

BARREL AND GAS CYLINDER GROUP.

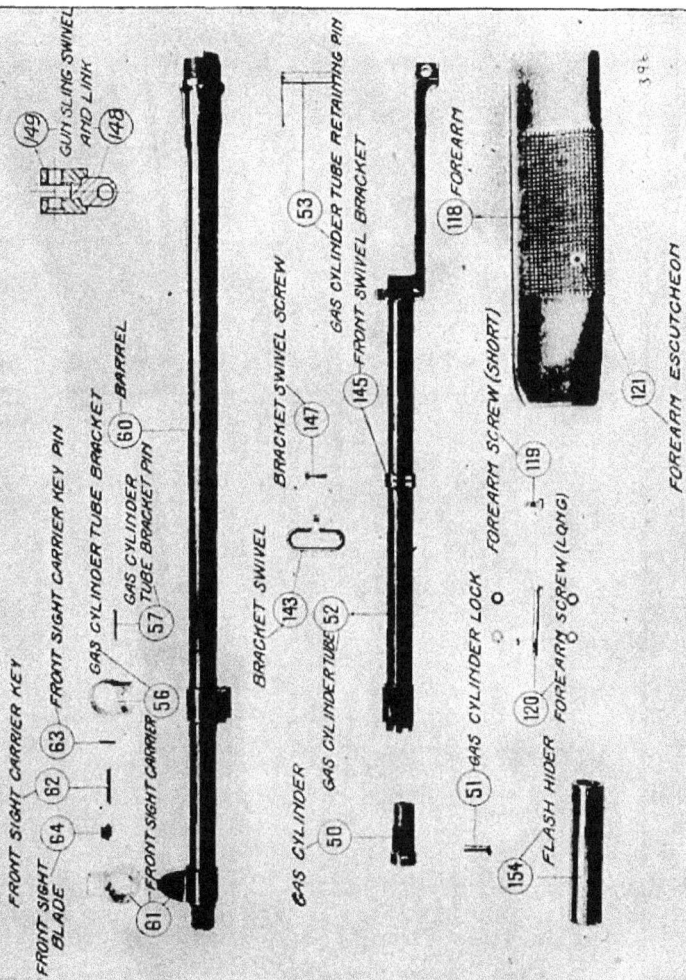

FRONT SIGHT CARRIER KEY

FRONT SIGHT CARRIER KEY PIN

GAS CYLINDER TUBE BRACKET

FRONT SIGHT BLADE

FRONT SIGHT CARRIER

GAS CYLINDER TUBE BRACKET PIN

GAS CYLINDER TUBE BRACKET

BARREL

(49) GUN SLING SWIVEL AND LINK

(48)

(149)

(63)

(62)

(64)

(61)

(56)

(57)

(60) BARREL

BRACKET SWIVEL SCREW

BRACKET SWIVEL

GAS CYLINDER

GAS CYLINDER TUBE

GAS CYLINDER TUBE RETAINING PIN

FRONT SWIVEL BRACKET

(53)

(147)

(143)

(52)

(50)

(145)

(118) FOREARM

FORE ARM SCREW (SHORT)

GAS CYLINDER LOCK

FORE ARM SCREW (LONG)

FLASH HIDER

FOREARM ESCUTCHEON

(119)

(120)

(51)

(154)

(121)

39¢

13

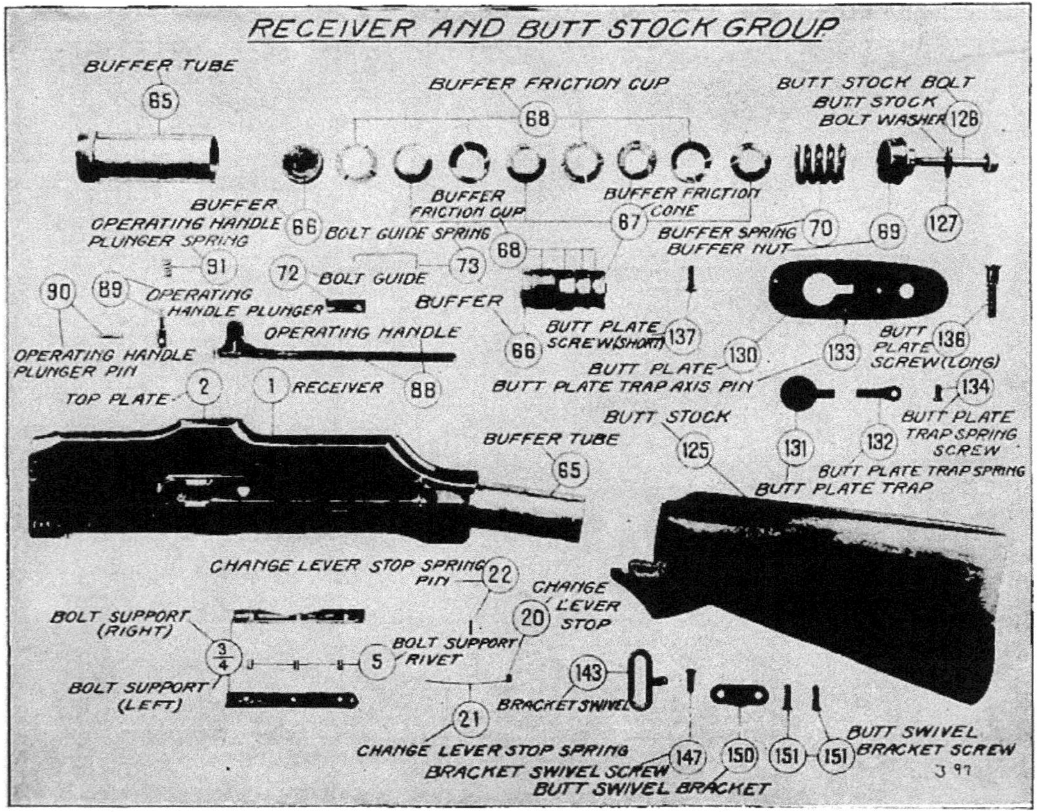

PLATE V.

RECEIVER AND BUTT STOCK GROUP

BUFFER TUBE

BUFFER FRICTION CUP

BUTT STOCK BOLT
BUTT STOCK
BOLT WASHER (126)

(127)

(69)

BUFFER SPRING (70)
BUFFER NUT

BUFFER FRICTION
CONE

(67) BUFFER SPRING AXIS PIN

BUTT PLATE (136)
SCREW (LONG)

(134)

BUTT PLATE
TRAP SPRING
SCREW

(133)

(132) BUTT PLATE TRAP SPRING

(131) BUTT PLATE TRAP

(130) BUTT PLATE
TRAP AXIS PIN

(137)

BUTT PLATE
SCREW (SHORT)

BUTT PLATE TRAP

(125) BUTT STOCK

(68)

BUFFER
FRICTION CUP

(68)

BOLT GUIDE SPRING

BUFFER
OPERATING HANDLE (66) BOLT GUIDE SPRING

(72) BOLT GUIDE

(73)

BUFFER

(66)

OPERATING HANDLE

(88)

(65) BUFFER TUBE

CHANGE
LEVER
STOP

(20)

BRACKET SWIVEL

BUTT SWIVEL
BRACKET SCREW

(151)

(151) (151)

(150)

(147) BUTT SWIVEL BRACKET

CHANGE LEVER STOP SCREW
BRACKET SWIVEL SCREW

(143)

BUFFER TUBE

BUFFER
OPERATING HANDLE (66) BOLT GUIDE SPRING

(31)
OPERATING
HANDLE PLUNGER SPRING

(89) OPERATING
HANDLE PLUNGER

(90)
OPERATING HANDLE
PLUNGER PIN

(2)

TOP PLATE

(1) RECEIVER

CHANGE LEVER STOP SPRING PIN (22)

BOLT SUPPORT
(RIGHT)

(5) RIVET

BOLT SUPPORT
(LEFT)

(3)
(4)

(21)

3 97

82. Link.
83. Link pin.
109. Magazine base.
32. Magazine catch.
35. Magazine catch pin (same as 14).
33. Magazine catch spring
114. Magazine filler.
110. Magazine follower.
34. Magazine release.
111. Magazine spring.
108. Magazine tube.
69. Operating handle plunger.
90. Operating handle plunger pin.
91. Operating handle plunger spring.
97. Rear sight axis screw.
98. Rear sight axis screw nut.
94. Rear sight base.
104. Rear sight leaf.
99. Rear sight slide.
100. Rear sight slide catch.
103. Rear sight slide catch axis pin.

101. Rear sight slide catch spring.
102. Rear sight slide stop screw.
95. Rear sight spring.
96. Rear sight spring screw.
1. Receiver.
40. Recoil spring.
41. Recoil spring guide.
42. Recoil spring guide head.
23. Sear.
25. Sear carrier.
24. Sear pin.
26. Sear spring.
19. Sear stop.
45. Slide.
2. Top plate.
13. Trigger.
10. Trigger guard.
11. Trigger guard retaining pin.
12. Trigger guard retaining pin handle.
14. Trigger pin (same as 35).

GROUP NOMENCLATURE.

9. Barrel and gas cylinder tube group (Plate IV):

50. Gas cylinder.
51. Gas cylinder lock.
52. Gas cylinder tube.
53. Gas cylinder tube retaining pin.
56. Gas cylinder tube bracket.
57. Gas cylinder tube bracket pin.
60. Barrel.
61. Front sight carrier.
62. Front sight carrier key.
63. Front sight carrier key pin.

64. Front sight blade.
118. Forearm (wood).
119. Forearm screw (short).
120. Forearm screw (long).
121. Forearm escutcheon.
143. Bracket swivel (2).
145. Front swivel bracket.
147. Bracket swivel screw (2).
154. Flash hider.
148–149. Gun sling swivel and link (2).

10. Receiver and butt stock group (Plate V):

1. Receiver.
2. Top plate.
3. Bolt support (right).
4. Bolt support (left).
5. Bolt support rivet (6).
20. Change lever stop.
21. Change lever stop spring.
22. Change lever stop spring pin.
65. Buffer tube.
66. Buffer.
67. Buffer friction cone (4).
68. Buffer friction cup (4).
69. Buffer nut.
70. Buffer spring.
72. Bolt guide.
73. Bolt guide spring.
88. Operating handle.

89. Operating handle plunger.
90. Operating handle plunger pin.
91. Operating handle plunger spring.
125. Butt stock.
126. Butt stock bolt.
127. Butt stock bolt washer.
130. Butt plate.
131. Butt plate trap.
132. Butt plate trap spring.
133. Butt plate trap axis pin.
134. Butt plate trap spring screw.
136. Butt plate screw (long).
137. Butt plate screw (short).
143. Bracket swivel (2).
147. Bracket swivel screw (2).
150. Butt swivel bracket.
151. Butt swivel bracket screw.

PLATE VI.

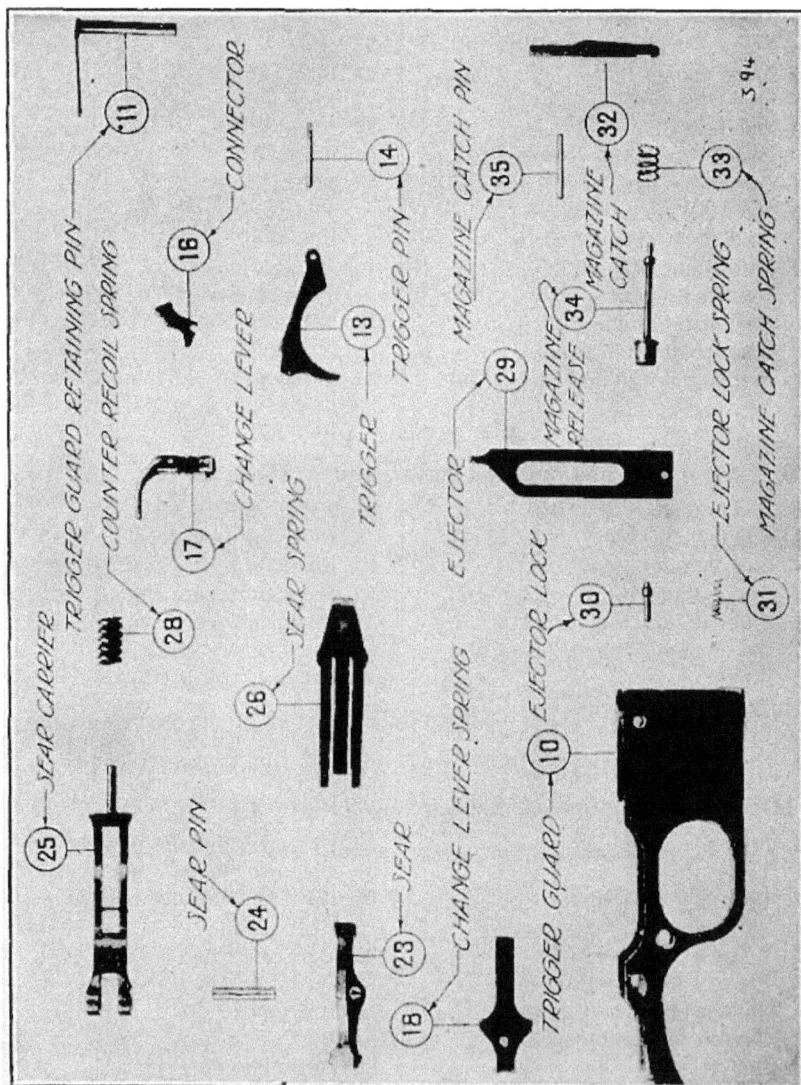

25 SEAR CARRIER

11 TRIGGER GUARD RETAINING PIN

28 COUNTER RECOIL SPRING

16 CONNECTOR

17 CHANGE LEVER

13 TRIGGER

14 TRIGGER PIN

35 MAGAZINE CATCH PIN

32

34 MAGAZINE CATCH

29 MAGAZINE RELEASE

33 MAGAZINE CATCH SPRING

31 EJECTOR LOCK SPRING

30 EJECTOR LOCK

10 EJECTOR

18 TRIGGER GUARD

26 SEAR SPRING

24 SEAR PIN

23 SEAR

CHANGE LEVER SPRING

394

TRIGGER-GUARD GROUP.

16

PLATE VII.

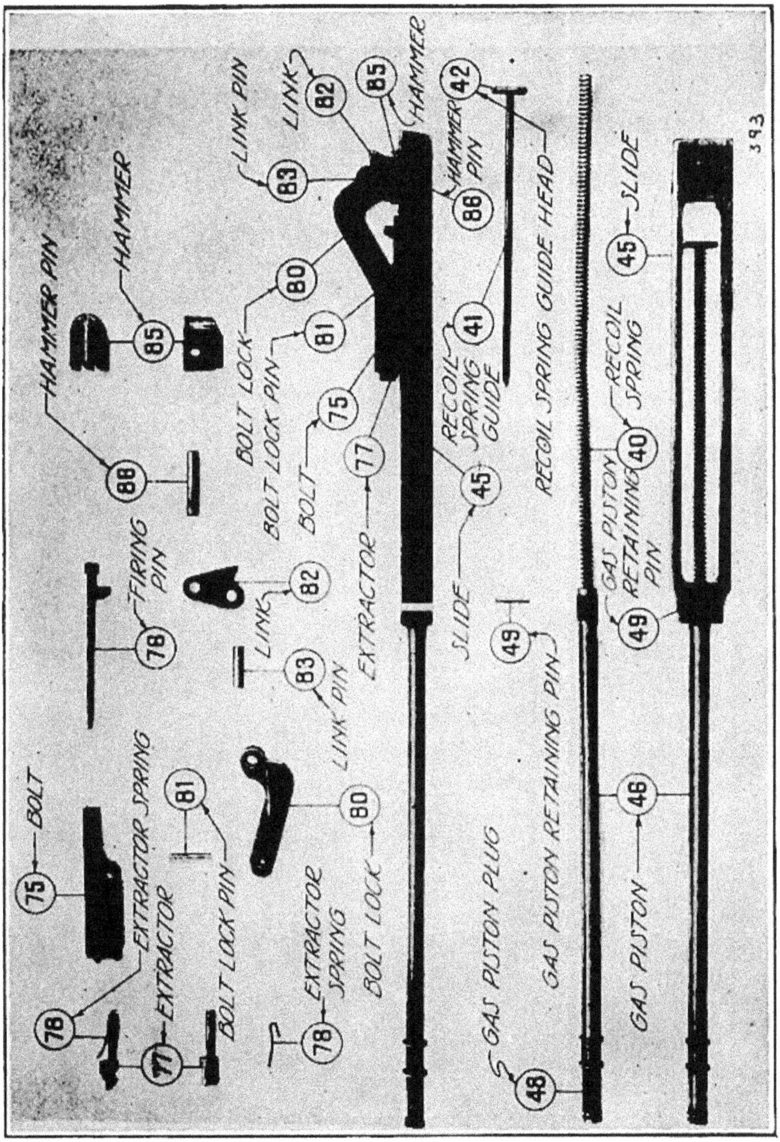

HAMMER PIN

HAMMER

LINK PIN

LINK

HAMMER

HAMMER PIN

BOLT LOCK

BOLT LOCK PIN

BOLT

EXTRACTOR

RECOIL SPRING GUIDE

RECOIL SPRING GUIDE HEAD

SLIDE

GAS PISTON RETAINING PIN

GAS PISTON PLUG

BOLT LOCK

EXTRACTOR SPRING

LINK PIN

LINK

EXTRACTOR

EXTRACTOR SPRING

FIRING PIN

BOLT

BOLT LOCK PIN

EXTRACTOR

GAS PISTON

GAS PISTON RETAINING PIN

RECOIL SPRING

SLIDE

OPERATING GROUP.

393

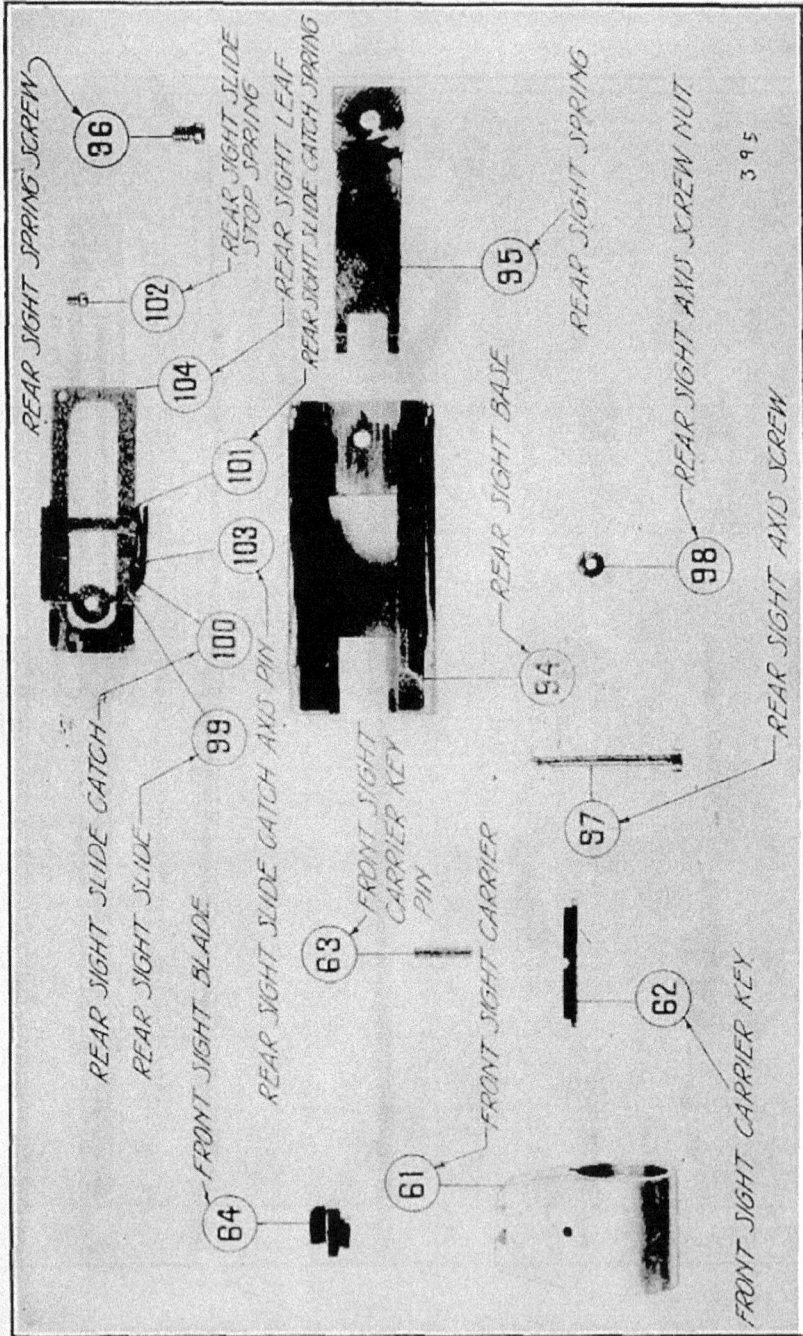

PLATE VIII.

18

REAR SIGHT SPRING SCREW

REAR SIGHT SLIDE STOP SPRING

REAR SIGHT LEAF

REAR SIGHT SLIDE CATCH SPRING

REAR SIGHT SPRING

REAR SIGHT AXIS SCREW NUT

REAR SIGHT AXIS SCREW

REAR SIGHT BLADE

REAR SIGHT SLIDE CATCH

REAR SIGHT SLIDE

FRONT SIGHT BLADE

REAR SIGHT SLIDE CATCH AXIS PIN

FRONT SIGHT CARRIER KEY PIN

FRONT SIGHT CARRIER

FRONT SIGHT CARRIER KEY

96

102

104

101

103

100

99

95

98

94

97

63

62

61

64

3 9 5

SIGHT GROUP.

PLATE IX.

GAS CYLINDER
CLEANING TOOL.

THONG CLEANER.

RUPTURED
CARTRIDGE
EXTRACTOR MARK II.

OIL CAN
MARK II.

COMBINATION TOOL.

SPARE PARTS CASE.

FABRIC CONTAINER - LARGE-
FOR SPARE PARTS.

FABRIC CONTAINER-SMALL-
FOR RECOIL SPRING.

MAGAZINE.

LUMINOUS SIGHTS
MARK III.

MAGAZINE FILLER

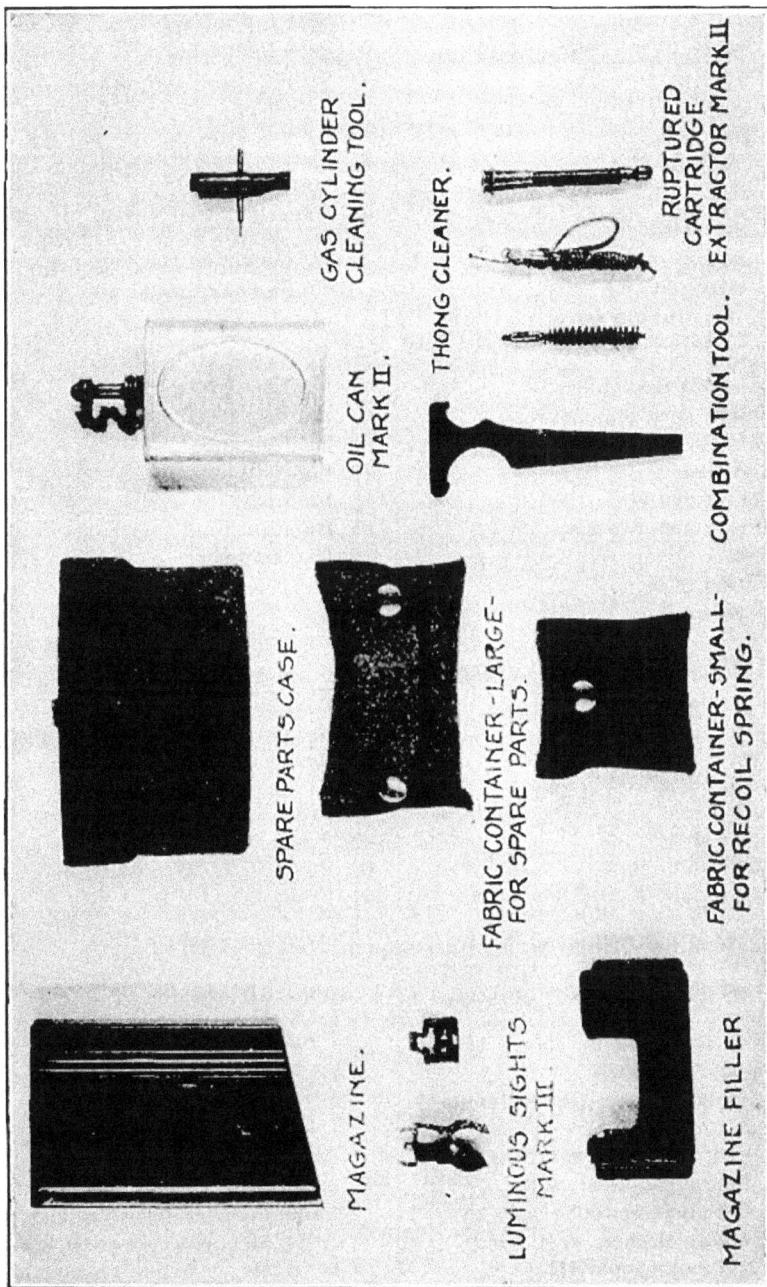

ACCESSORIES AND SPARE PARTS GROUP.

11. Trigger guard group (Plate VI):

10. Trigger guard.
11. Trigger guard retaining pin.
13. Trigger.
14. Trigger pin (same as 35).
16. Connector.
17. Change lever.
18. Change lever spring.
19. Sear stop.
23. Sear.
24. Sear pin.

25. Sear carrier.
26. Sear spring.
28. Counter-recoil spring.
29. Ejector.
30. Ejector lock.
31. Ejector lock spring.
32. Magazine catch.
33. Magazine catch spring.
34. Magazine release.
35. Magazine catch pin (same as 14).

12. Operating group (Plate VII):

40. Recoil spring.
41. Recoil spring guide.
43. Recoil spring guide head.
45. Slide.
46. Gas piston.
47. Gas piston plug.
49. Gas piston retaining pin.
75. Bolt.
76. Firing pin.

77. Extractor.
78. Extractor spring.
80. Bolt lock.
81. Bolt lock pin.
82. Link.
83. Link pin.
85. Hammer.
86. Hammer pin.

13. Sight group (Plate VIII):

Rear sight group:
94. Rear sight base.
95. Rear sight spring.
96. Rear sight spring screw.
97. Rear sight axis screw.
98. Rear sight axis screw nut..
99. Rear sight slide.
100. Rear sight slide catch.
101. Rear sight slide catch spring.

Rear sight group:
102. Rear sight slide stop screw.
103. Rear sight slide catch axis pin.
104. Rear sight leaf.
Front sight group:
61. Front sight carrier.
62. Front sight carrier key.
63. Front sight carrier key pin.
64. Front sight blade.

14. Field spare parts and accessories (Plate IX):

71 Magazines.
3 Magazine fillers.
1 Set luminous sights (Mark III) in box.
1 Spare parts case, leather, containing:
   1 Fabric container, large.
   1 Fabric container, small.
   1 Combination tool.
   1 Thong cleaner.
   1 Oil can (Mark II).
   1 Gas cylinder cleaning tool.
   1 Ruptured cartridge extractor (Mark II).

1 Spare parts case, etc.—Continued.
   1 Extractor (77).
   1 Extractor spring (78).
   1 Recoil spring (40).
   2 Firing pins (76).
   1 Sear spring (26).
   1 Connector (16).
   1 Magazine catch spring (33).
   1 Gas cylinder tube retaining pin (53).
   1 Trigger guard retaining pin (11).

METHODS OF INSTRUCTION.

15. In the company or platoon all men should be combined in one class under one or more commissioned instructors. Each sergeant will supervise his own section as assistant instructor, and each corporal will act as instructor for his own squad.

It is contemplated that the sergeants and corporals shall have had a thorough course of instruction prior to their men.

If possible a classroom should be provided with a blackboard, seats for the entire class, and one rifle table per squad, sufficiently large to permit the entire squad to be grouped around it while working on the rifle.

SUBJECTS.

16. Mechanism will be taught by subjects in the following order:

(1) Stripping and assembling of rifle, except trigger mechanism.

(2) Stripping and assembling of trigger mechanism.

(3) Stripping and assembling of magazine.

(4) Functioning of gun proper, including the magazine.

(5) Functioning of the trigger mechanism.

(6) Accessories and spare parts.

(7) Stoppages and immediate action (classroom).

(8) Care and preservation.

NOTE.—Stoppages and immediate action will be practically taught on the range during the marksmanship course.

DETAILED METHOD OF INSTRUCTION.

17. No discussion of functioning should be permitted prior to the completion of stripping and assembling. Nomenclature will be learned during the instruction of stripping and assembling and reviewed throughout the remainder of the course.

In each subject the following procedure will be observed:

INTRODUCTION.

The instructor will preface his instruction with a brief general lecture leading up to the specific subject in hand. He must provide ahead of time all material needed for the day's work.

EXPLANATORY DEMONSTRATION.

The instructor will make a detailed explanation of the subject to be taught, illustrating or demonstrating his explanation as he proceeds. This explanatory demonstration will be made to the class as a whole; this results in uniform instruction for the entire class in the beginning of each subject.

IMITATION.

All men will repair to their rifles and each man in turn will imitate the explanatory demonstration of his instructor. The other members of the team will stand by with handbooks and check up any errors.

PRACTICE.

All men will then practice the particular operations in hand until they become proficient. The instructor will supervise this work, correct errors, assist backward men, and give detailed instruction in general. As men deem themselves qualified they will report to their instructor for examination. He will require a perfect recitation before reporting a man qualified to the senior instructor.

INTERROGATION.

Men will frequently be examined as to their knowledge of the work in hand. Questions will be framed with a view to bringing out important points. This interrogation should be followed wherever possible throughout the remainder of the course.

SCHEDULE OF INSTRUCTION.

18. Mechanism should be taught in a series of lessons which should include all the instructional matter which follows. The subject included in each lesson will depend upon the degree of intelligence of the class and the length of the period allotted. Each lesson should be mastered by the majority of the class prior to proceeding to the next, and whenever possible the preceding lesson should be reviewed with the current one.

Men should be encouraged to ask questions at all times, without, however, going ahead of the subject in hand.

CLASSROOM REGULATIONS.

19. The following regulations should be observed in the classroom during stripping and assembling:
  (1) Force will not be used.
  (2) The piece will not be stripped nor assembled against time.
  (3) Magazines will be carefully handled and every precaution taken to prevent denting or bending.

STRIPPING AND ASSEMBLING.

INTRODUCTION.

20. The instructor will give a brief talk introducing the rifle, wherein he will cover its type, caliber, characteristics, and any such other points of general interest as he deems advisable. He will then go over the rifle, naming and describing the various parts externally visible. This he will follow by slowly stripping the rifle, exclusive of the trigger mechanism and buffer, holding up, naming, and describing each part as he removes it. He will call attention to all cams, locks, slots, profiles, and springs, but will not at this time describe their function. The instructor will assemble the piece according to the same procedure. After this explanatory demonstration, the teams being assembled at their rifles, the instructor will describe, step by step, how to strip and assemble the rifle, naming and describing parts as before. He will require one man at each rifle to imitate him as he finishes, describing each step, the remaining members of the team observing. Every man in the class will repeat names as called out by the instructor. No one will be permitted to go ahead of this explanation and assistants will keep the backward men up with the explanation.

SEQUENCE AND METHOD OF STRIPPING.

21. (1) Cock the piece.
    (2) Gas cylinder tube retaining pin.
    (3) Gas cylinder tube (let mechanism forward easily).
    (4) Trigger-guard retaining pin.
    (5) Trigger guard.
    (6) Recoil spring guide and recoil spring.
    (7) Hammer pin through hammer pin hole in receiver.
    (8) Operating handle.
    (9) Hammer pin.
   (10) Hammer.
   (11) Slide.
   (12) Bolt guide pushed out.
   (13) Bolt, bolt lock, and link.
   (14) Firing pin.
   (15) Extractor.

22. Lay the rifle on the table, barrel down, pointing to the left.

Cock the piece. This must be done in order that the gas cylinder tube may clear the gas piston and gas cylinder bracket, female.

Remove the gas cylinder tube retaining pin by turning the handle 90° in a clockwise direction and lift out.

Remove gas cylinder tube.

Let the slide forward very *easily* in order to release the tension of the recoil spring and avoid any damage to the rifle. Care must be taken during stripping and assembling to avoid working against tension of any springs.

Remove the trigger guard retaining pin by turning handle 90° in a clockwise direction and lifting out.

LAY THE PIECE BARREL DOWN AND POINTING TO THE LEFT, THE PIECE RESTING ON THE BARREL AND REAR SIGHT

(1)

COCK THE PIECE, AND PUSH OPERATING HANDLE FORWARD

(2)

WITH POINT OF CARTRIDGE UNLOCK THE GAS CYLINDER TUBE RETAINING PIN....

(3)

SWING IT UPWARD....

(4)

...AND WITHDRAW IT TO THE RIGHT.

(5)

REMOVE THE GAS CYLINDER TUBE AND FOREARM TO THE FRONT OVER THE PISTON......

(6)

...WITH THE MIDDLE AND INDEX FINGERS OF LEFT HAND ASTRIDE THE PISTON--AGAINST THE FORWARD END OF THE SLIDE ....

(7)

...PULL THE TRIGGER WITH THE THUMB OF THE RIGHT HAND ....

(8)

AND LET THE MECHANISM MOVE GENTLY FORWARD.... RESISTING THE PRESSURE OF THE RECOIL SPRING WITH THE FINGERS ASTRIDE THE GAS PISTON

(9)

UNLOCK AND REMOVE THE TRIGGER GUARD RETAINING PIN AS SHOWN IN PLATES 3,4 & 5.

(10)

REMOVE THE TRIGGER GUARD

(11)

PLACE END OF INDEX FINGER ON CHECKERED END OF RECOIL SPRING GUIDE HEAD...TURN IT UNTIL DISENGAGED FROM ITS RETAINING SHOULDERS

(12)

.... AND REMOVE THE RECOIL SPRING AND GUIDE TO THE REAR

(13)

NOW WITH THE POINT OF A CARTRIDGE INSERTED IN THE DISMOUNTING HOLE IN THE OPERATING HANDLE ..

(14)

.... AND THE FOREFINGER OF THE LEFT HAND PUSHING GENTLY BACKWARD ON THE OPERATING HANDLE

(15)

EXERT PRESSURE WITH CARTRIDGE POINT TO THE LEFT SO THAT WHEN THE HAMMER PIN AND THE DISMOUNTING HOLE IN RECEIVER COINCIDE.....

DISMOUNTING HOLE

(16)

17 ...THE END OF THE HAMMER PIN WILL BE FORCED THROUGH THE DISMOUNTING HOLE ...

18 NOW REMOVE THE OPERATING HANDLE TO THE REAR...

19 REMOVE THE HAMMER PIN TO THE LEFT...

20 HOOK THE INDEX FINGER OF THE LEFT HAND UNDER THE FRONT END OF THE HAMMER AND LIFT IT OUT, OR PULL THE SLIDE FORWARD AND QUICKLY PUSH IT TO THE REAR, SHAKING OUT THE HAMMER

21 SWING THE LINK BACK AND

22 REMOVE THE SLIDE TO THE FRONT

23 GRASP THE LINK WITH THE THUMB AND FINGER OF THE RIGHT HAND AND LIFT THE BOLT LOCK OUT OF ENGAGEMENT WITH ITS SEAT IN TOP OF RECEIVER, SLIDING IT REARWARD AS FAR AS IT WILL GO. BOLT GUIDE

24 STILL HOLDING THE LINK, PRESS OUTWARD ON THE BOLT GUIDE WITH END OF LEFT THUMB (OR POINT OF BULLET) AND LIFT THE BOLT OUT.

25 LIFT THE BOLT LOCK AND REMOVE THE FIRING PIN ...

26 ...USING THE FIRING PIN AS A DRIFT, PUSH OUT THE LINK PIN.

27 PLACE A BULLET NOSE UNDER THE CLAW OF THE EXTRACTOR, PUSH OUT UNTIL EXTRACTOR SHOULDER IS CLEAR...

28 ...THEN PRY THE EXTRACTOR FORWARD......

29 ...AND REMOVE IT FROM THE BOLT.

30 PULL OUT THE EXTRACTOR SPRING. NOTE. THE PIECE IS NOW DISMOUNTED AS FAR AS IS ALLOWED IN FIELD DISMOUNTING.

Lift out the trigger guard group.

Remove the recoil spring guide by pressing the right index finger on the checkered surface of its head and turning it until the ends are clear of the retaining shoulders. This may also be done by using the index finger of the left hand and the middle finger of the right hand.

Line up the hammer pin holes on the receiver and the operating handle by inserting the point of the recoil spring guide or dummy cartridge in the hole on the operating handle with the right hand, press against the hammer pin and push the slide backward with the left hand. The recoil spring guide will push the hammer pin through its hole in the receiver as the hammer pin registers with the latter.

Remove the operating handle by pulling straight to the rear.

Push the hammer forward out of its seat in the slide and lift out of the receiver.

Remove the slide by pulling forward out of the receiver, being careful that the link is pushed well down, thus allowing the slide to clear. In removing the slide take care to avoid striking the gas piston or rings against the gas cylinder tube bracket, female.

Force the bolt guide out with the left thumb or point of bullet.

Lift out the bolt, bolt lock, and link by pulling slowly to rear end of receiver and up.

Pull out the firing pin from its way in the bolt.

Remove the extractor by pressing the small end of a dummy cartridge against the claw and exerting pressure upward and to the front.

SEQUENCE AND METHOD OF ASSEMBLING.

23. (1) Extractor.
    (2) Firing pin.
    (3) Bolt, bolt lock, and link.
    (4) Slide.
    (5) Hammer.
    (6) Hammer pin (far enough to register all holes).
    (7) Operating handle.
    (8) Hammer pin fully seated.
    (9) Recoil spring and guide.
  (10) Trigger guard.
  (11) Trigger guard retaining pin.
  (12) Cock the piece.
  (13) Gas cylinder tube.
  (14) Gas cylinder tube retaining pin.
  (15) Let slide forward easily.
  (16) Test the piece.

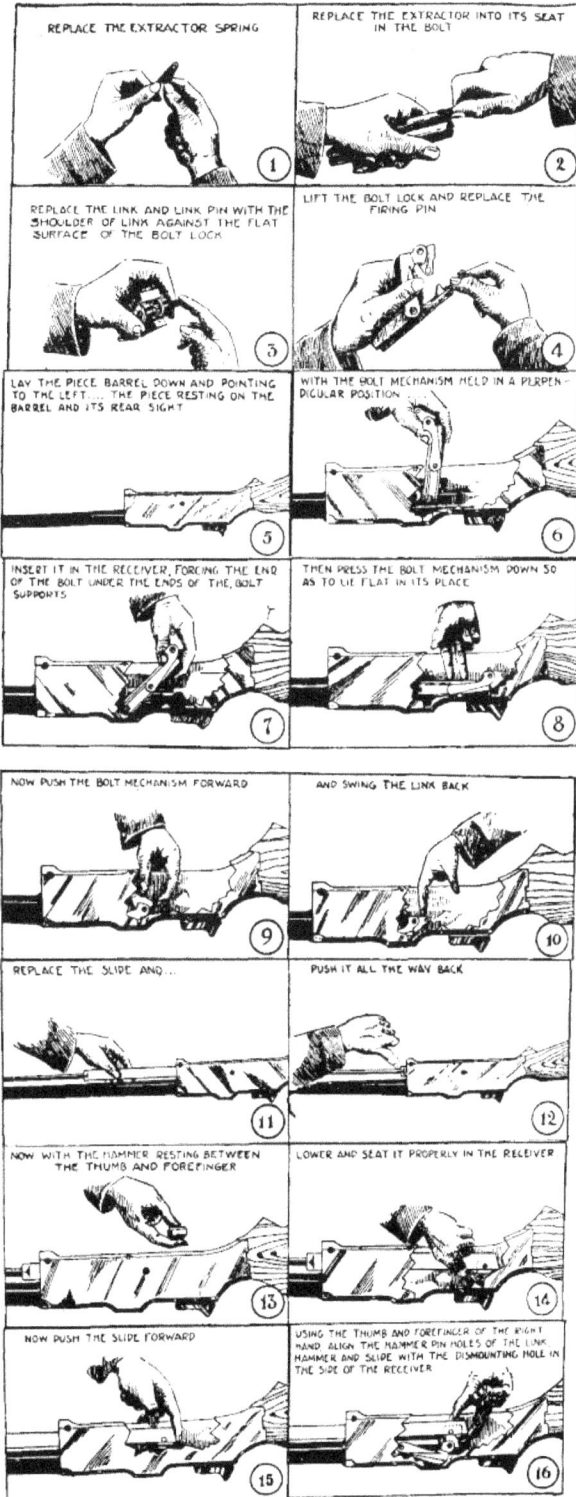

1. REPLACE THE EXTRACTOR SPRING

2. REPLACE THE EXTRACTOR INTO ITS SEAT IN THE BOLT

3. REPLACE THE LINK AND LINK PIN WITH THE SHOULDER OF LINK AGAINST THE FLAT SURFACE OF THE BOLT LOCK

4. LIFT THE BOLT LOCK AND REPLACE THE FIRING PIN

5. LAY THE PIECE BARREL DOWN AND POINTING TO THE LEFT.... THE PIECE RESTING ON THE BARREL AND ITS REAR SIGHT

6. WITH THE BOLT MECHANISM HELD IN A PERPENDICULAR POSITION

7. INSERT IT IN THE RECEIVER, FORCING THE END OF THE BOLT UNDER THE ENDS OF THE BOLT SUPPORTS

8. THEN PRESS THE BOLT MECHANISM DOWN SO AS TO LIE FLAT IN ITS PLACE

9. NOW PUSH THE BOLT MECHANISM FORWARD

10. AND SWING THE LINK BACK

11. REPLACE THE SLIDE AND...

12. PUSH IT ALL THE WAY BACK

13. NOW WITH THE HAMMER RESTING BETWEEN THE THUMB AND FOREFINGER

14. LOWER AND SEAT IT PROPERLY IN THE RECEIVER

15. NOW PUSH THE SLIDE FORWARD

16. USING THE THUMB AND FOREFINGER OF THE RIGHT HAND ALIGN THE HAMMER PIN HOLES OF THE LINK, HAMMER AND SLIDE WITH THE DISMOUNTING HOLE IN THE SIDE OF THE RECEIVER

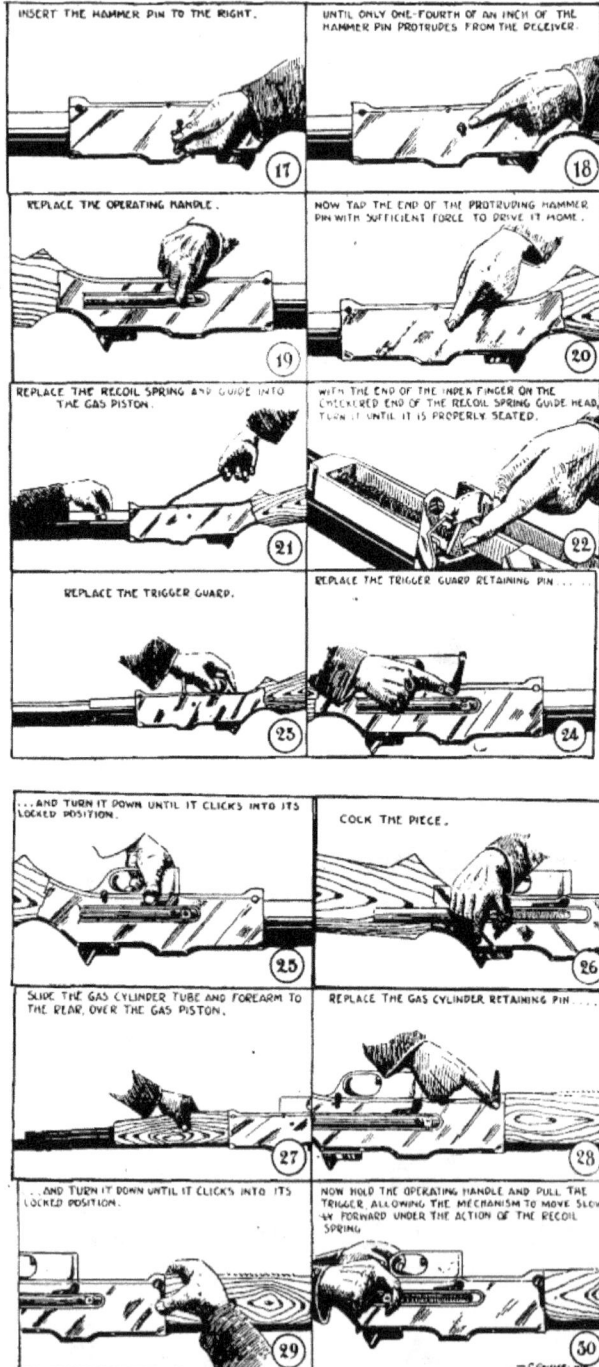

INSERT THE HAMMER PIN TO THE RIGHT.

17

UNTIL ONLY ONE-FOURTH OF AN INCH OF THE HAMMER PIN PROTRUDES FROM THE RECEIVER.

18

REPLACE THE OPERATING HANDLE.

19

NOW TAP THE END OF THE PROTRUDING HAMMER PIN WITH SUFFICIENT FORCE TO DRIVE IT HOME.

20

REPLACE THE RECOIL SPRING AND GUIDE INTO THE GAS PISTON.

21

WITH THE END OF THE INDEX FINGER ON THE CHECKERED END OF THE RECOIL SPRING GUIDE HEAD, TURN IT UNTIL IT IS PROPERLY SEATED.

22

REPLACE THE TRIGGER GUARD.

23

REPLACE THE TRIGGER GUARD RETAINING PIN . . . . .

24

. . . AND TURN IT DOWN UNTIL IT CLICKS INTO ITS LOCKED POSITION.

25

COCK THE PIECE.

26

SLIDE THE GAS CYLINDER TUBE AND FOREARM TO THE REAR, OVER THE GAS PISTON.

27

REPLACE THE GAS CYLINDER RETAINING PIN . . . . .

28

. . . AND TURN IT DOWN UNTIL IT CLICKS INTO ITS LOCKED POSITION.

29

NOW HOLD THE OPERATING HANDLE AND PULL THE TRIGGER, ALLOWING THE MECHANISM TO MOVE SLOW-LY FORWARD UNDER THE ACTION OF THE RECOIL SPRING.

30

24. Replace extractor spring.

Replace extractor into its seat in the bolt.

Place the link and link pin with the shoulder of the link against the flat surface of the bolt lock.

Lift the bolt lock and replace the firing pin.

Lay the piece barrel down and pointing to the left so that the piece is resting on the barrel and rear sight.

With the bolt mechanism held in a perpendicular position, insert it in the receiver, forcing the end of the bolt under the ends of the bolt supports, and then press the bolt mechanism down so as to lie flat in its place.

Push the bolt mechanism forward, swing the link down, then replace the slide and push it all the way back.

With the hammer resting between the thumb and the forefinger, lower and seat it properly in the receiver and push the slide forward.

With the thumb and forefinger of the right hand, align the hammer pin holes of the link, hammer, and slide with the hammer pin hole in the side of the receiver.

Insert hammer pin to the right until only one-fourth of an inch of the hammer pin protrudes from the receiver.

Replace the operating handle.

Tap the end of the protruding hammer pin with sufficient force to drive it home.

Replace recoil spring and guide.

With the end of the index finger on the checkered end of the recoil spring guide head, turn it until it is properly seated.

Replace the trigger guard and trigger guard retaining pin.

Cock the piece.

Slide the gas cylinder tube and forearm to the rear of the gas piston.

Replace gas cylinder tube retaining pin.

Test the piece.

25. When this demonstration has been completed once, the remaining members of the squad will strip and assemble the piece, naming and describing each part as it is removed. The other members of the team will stand by with handbooks and correct any errors of nomenclature or method of stripping and assembling. Instructors will supervise and assist students and will see that mistakes are corrected as they are made. They will examine men whom they believe to be qualified and report to the senior instructor those who make perfect recitations.

STRIPPING AND ASSEMBLING BLINDFOLDED.

26. After all men become thoroughly proficient in stripping and assembling, and if time permits, they should be required to strip and assemble the rifle blindfolded. Instructors supervise this instruction to prevent wrong assembly or forcing of parts. Assistance should be given if necessary. If any part is called for by its right name, same will be furnished.

The other members of the squad not blindfolded will have various parts put in their hands while placed so they can not see what these parts are and will be required to identify them by feel. Extraneous pieces of metal may be introduced in this latter exercise.

The purpose of this instruction is to so train the soldier as to enable him to replace breakages and reduce stoppages in the dark.

TO REMOVE FIRING PIN OR EXTRACTOR WITHOUT STRIPPING THE RIFLE.

27. After removing the trigger guard, turn the piece over with the barrel up. Keep the bolt guide free of the bolt by inserting the base of a dummy cartridge underneath it after it has been pushed out. Draw the operating handle to the rear until the bolt mechanism drops clear of the receiver. Let the mechanism forward and turn the gun so that the bottom will be upward. With the left hand hold the bolt and withdraw firing pin with right hand.

To assemble, replace the firing pin, draw the mechanism to the rear, place the face of the bolt under the bolt supports and press down the firing pin until bolt clears the bolt guide. Let the mechanism forward and replace the trigger mechanism.

TO REMOVE EXTRACTOR.

28. Draw back mechanism and insert empty case or dummy cartridge between bolt head and chamber, exposing the extractor.

With the forefinger of the left hand force out the claw of the extractor, then place point of cartridge behind the extractor shoulder and pry forward until extractor is free of the recess.

Remove extractor spring.

With the thumb and forefinger of the left hand insert extractor into extractor recess in bolt and force it to the rear until it is in position. Draw operating handle to the rear and shake out empty case.

STRIPPING AND ASSEMBLING TRIGGER MECHANISM.

SEQUENCE AND METHOD OF STRIPPING AND ASSEMBLING.

29. This stripping and assembling is not to be done in the field except to replace breakages:

    (1) Ejector.
    (2) Magazine catch spring.
    (3) Magazine catch pin.

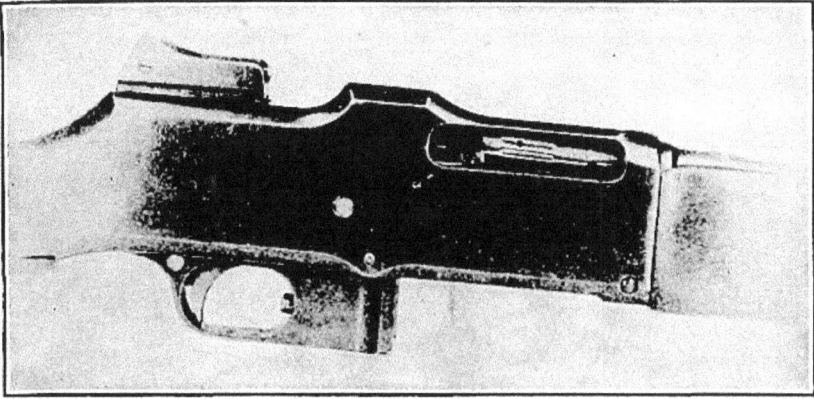

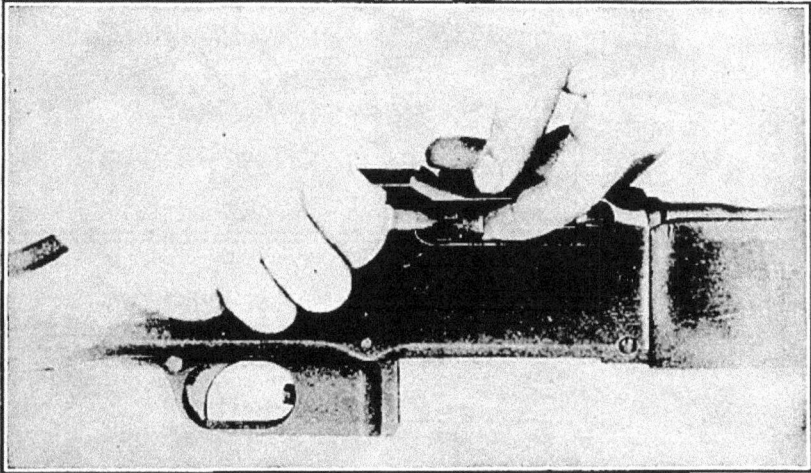

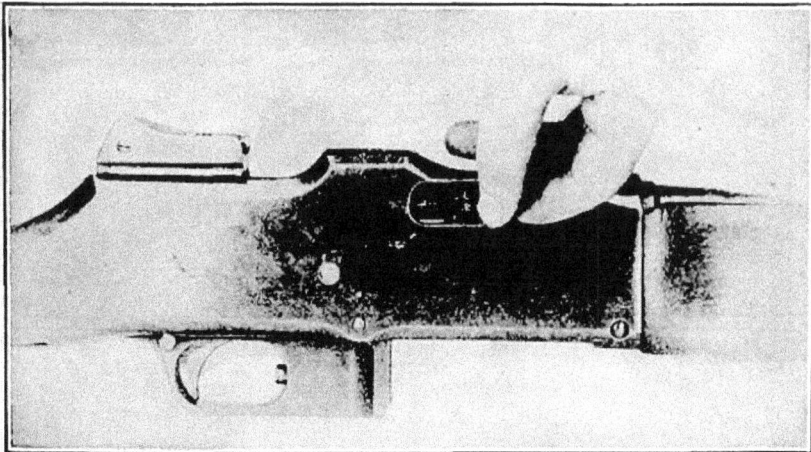

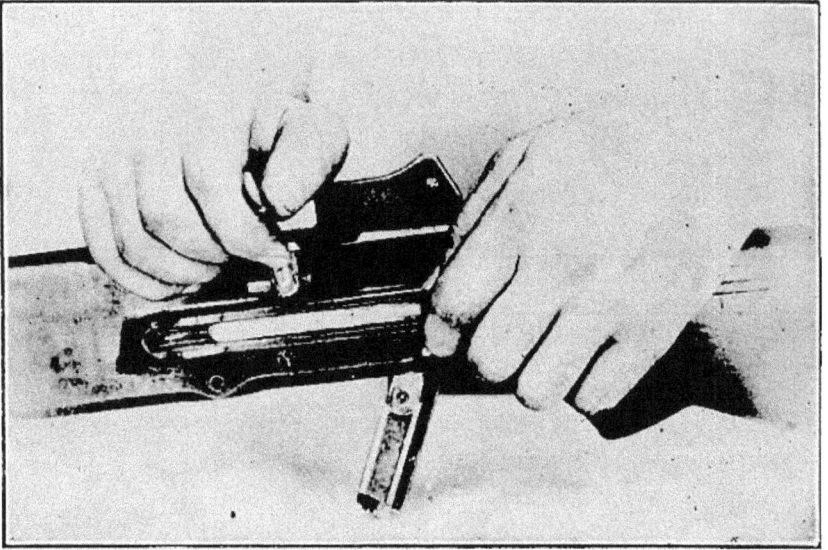

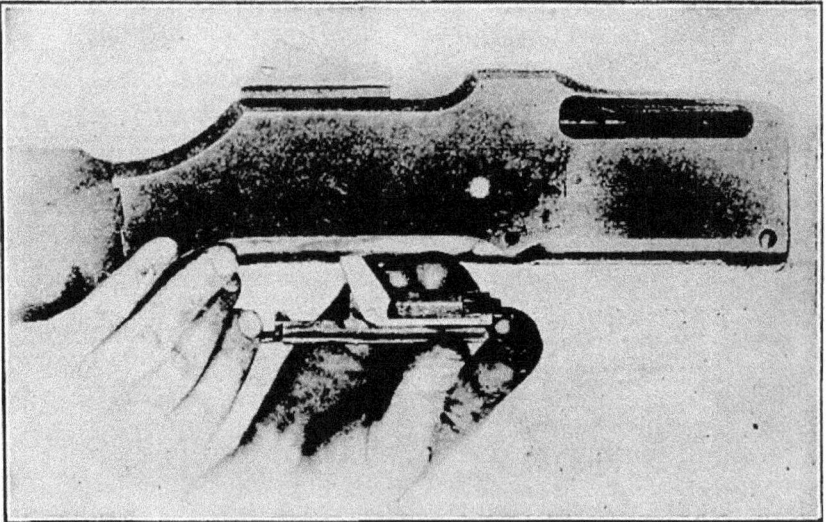

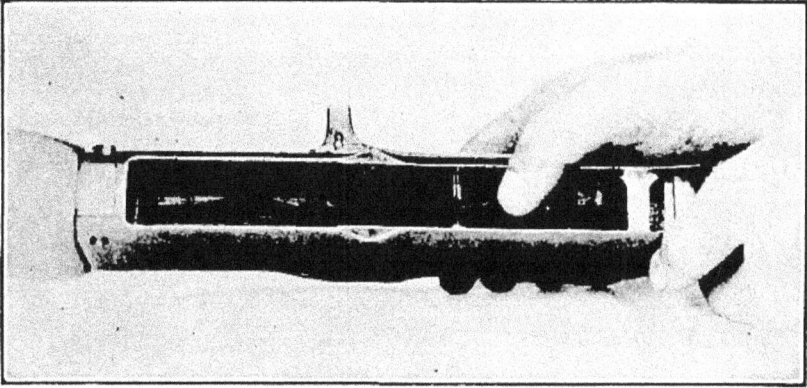

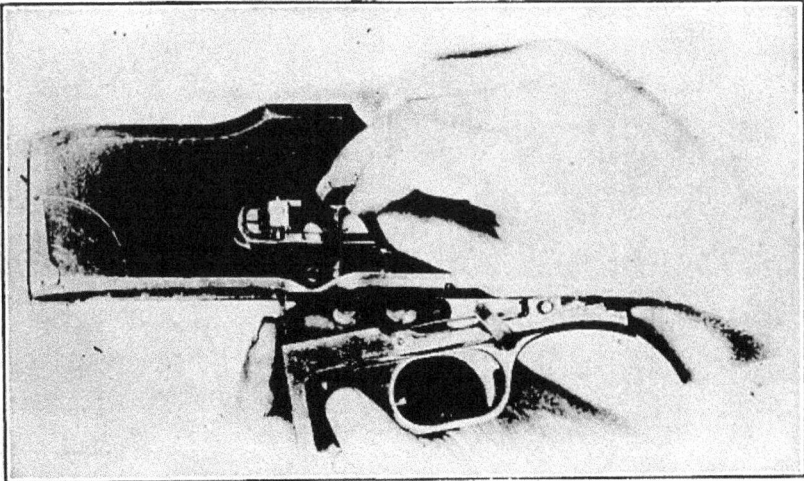

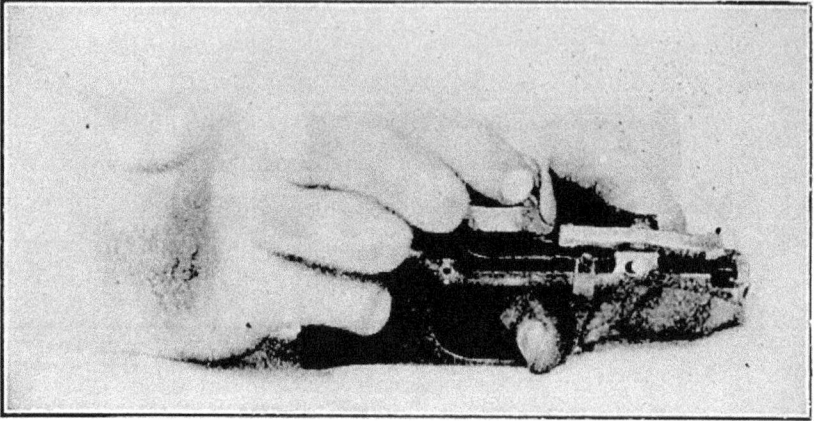

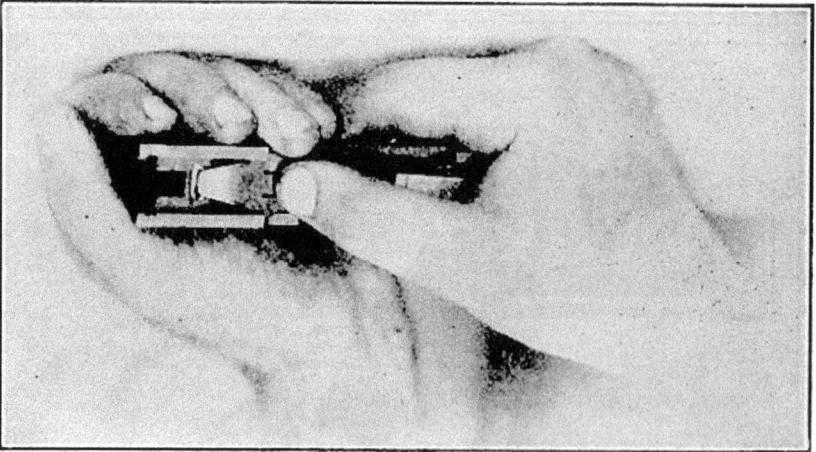

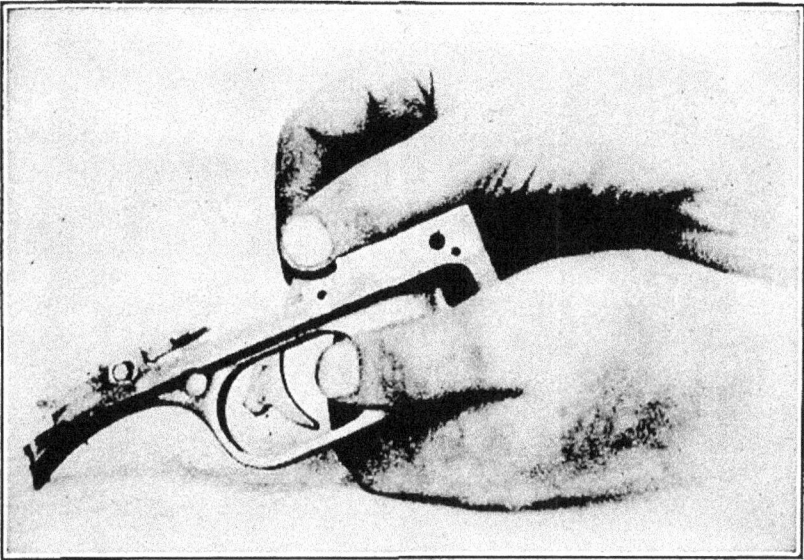

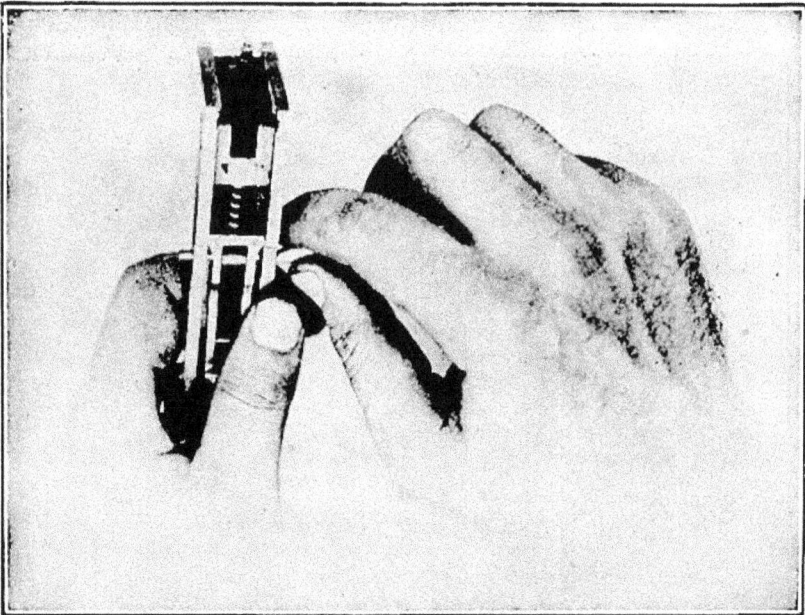

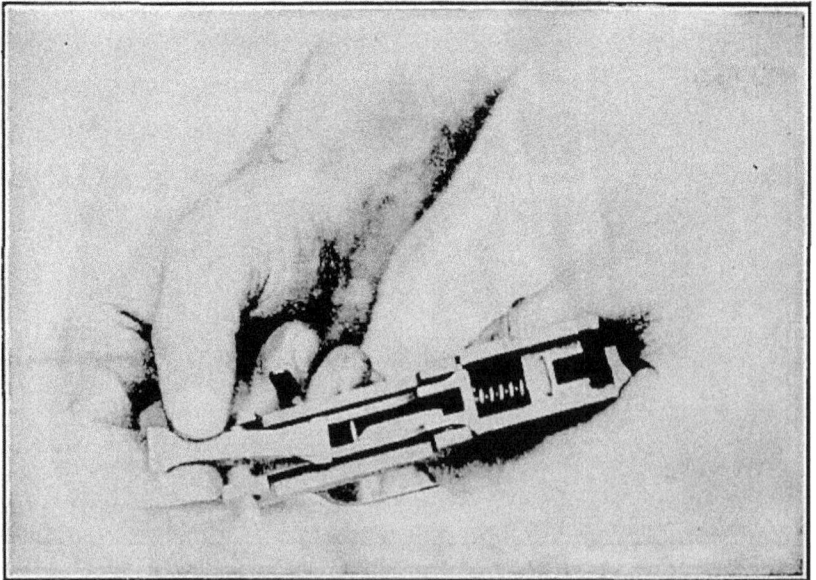

   (4) Magazine catch.

   (5) Magazine release.

   (6) Sear spring.

   (7) Trigger pin.

   (8) Trigger and connector.

   (9) Sear pin.

  (10) Sear.

  (11) Sear carrier and counter-recoil spring.

  (12) Change lever spring.

  (13) Change lever.

30. Depress the ejector lock with the point of a dummy cartridge. Hold the thumb in front of the magazine catch spring to prevent it flying out and slide the ejector out of its seat. Remove the magazine catch spring. Remove the magazine catch pin and then the magazine catch and magazine release may be lifted out.

To remove sear spring, insert the handle of the trigger guard retaining pin under the sear spring above the connector stop, pry up, pressing against sear spring with thumb and pulling it out to the rear. Push out the trigger pin to the right or left and then the trigger and connector will fall out.

Push out sear pin with recoil spring guide. Remove sear. Pry up on sear carrier and lift out.

Change lever spring is removed by prying the bent over rear end out of its seat with the rounded end of the sear spring and moving the change lever from front to rear. When clear of the change lever it is pushed the rest of the way out by pressing with the thumb against the sear stop.

Change lever is pulled out.

31. Sequence of assembling is in reverse order of stripping.

The following points should be observed in assembling:

(1) It is easy to seat the magazine catch spring if the ejector is moved down until it is flush with the magazine catch spring before attempting to compress the latter.

(2) In assembling the change lever spring, first insert the ears in the slots in the trigger guard and push spring forward a slight distance, then insert the rounded end of the sear spring between the rear end of the trigger guard and the change lever spring. By prying up with the sear spring and at the same time pressing against sear stop with thumb and rotating change lever from rear to front the change lever spring is easily seated. Sear carrier and counter-recoil spring are assembled to trigger mechanism by inserting counter-recoil spring guide in the seat, then using the recoil spring guide as a lever in the sear pin hole, prying the sear carrier forward until its rear end is held by the ears on the change lever spring.

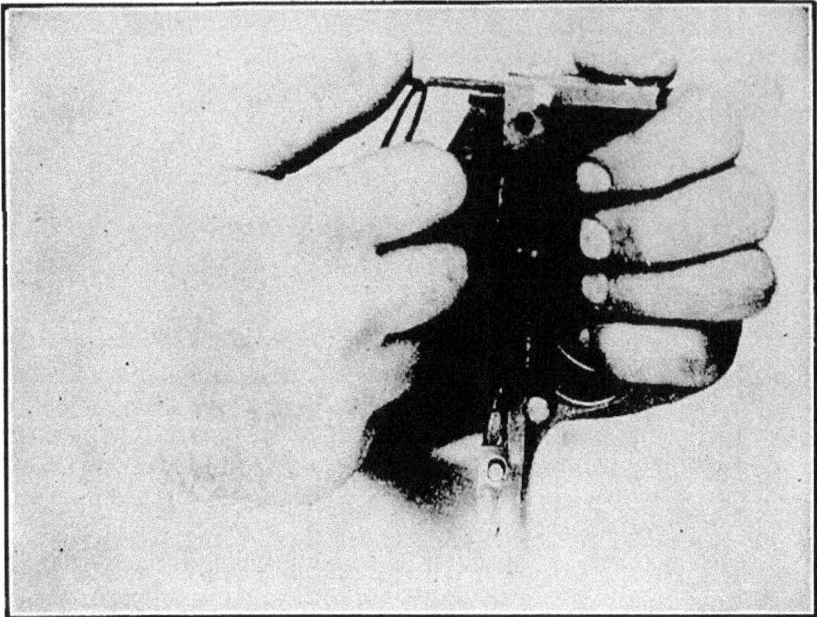

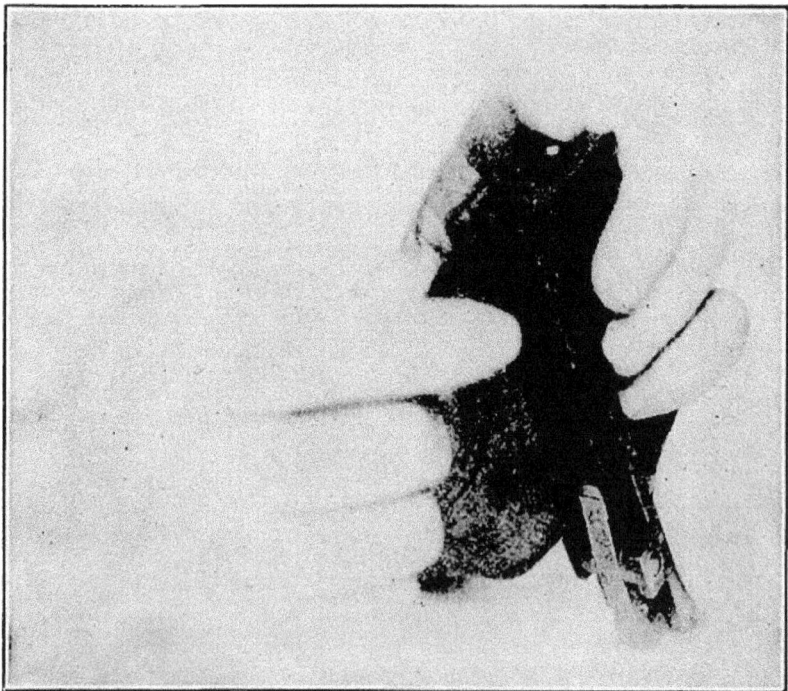

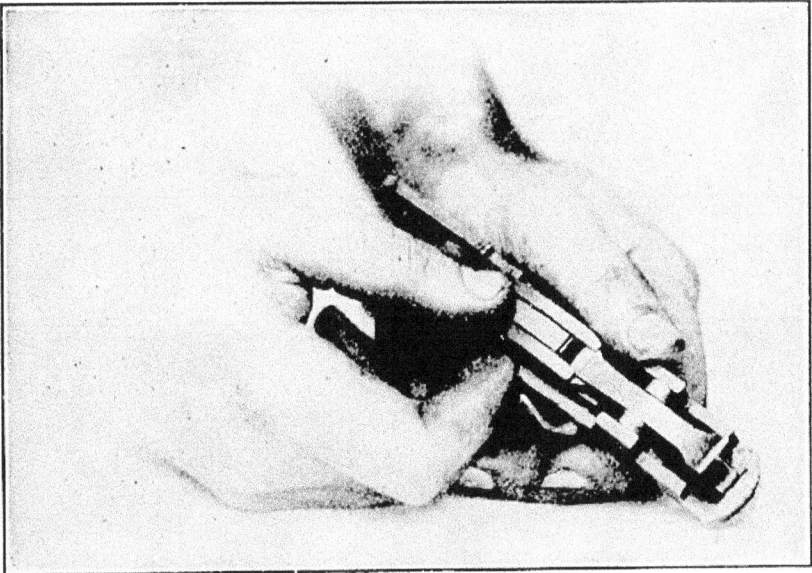

39

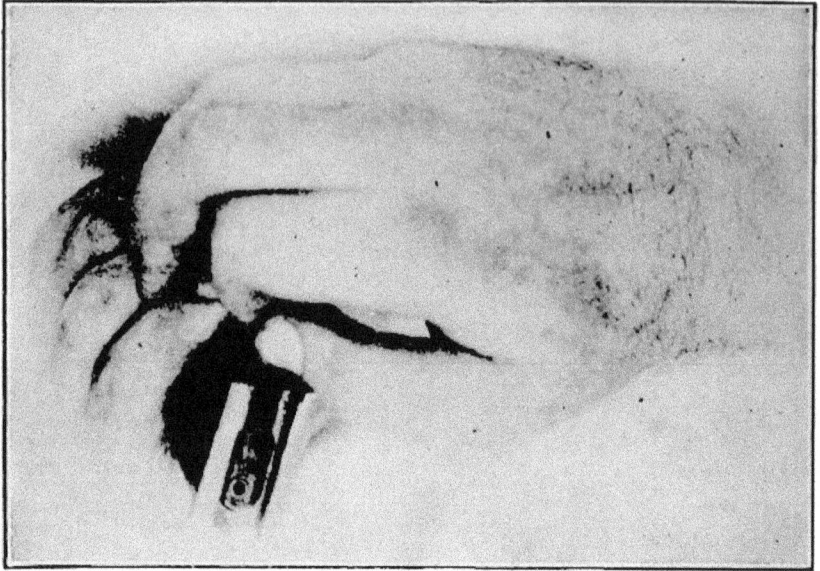

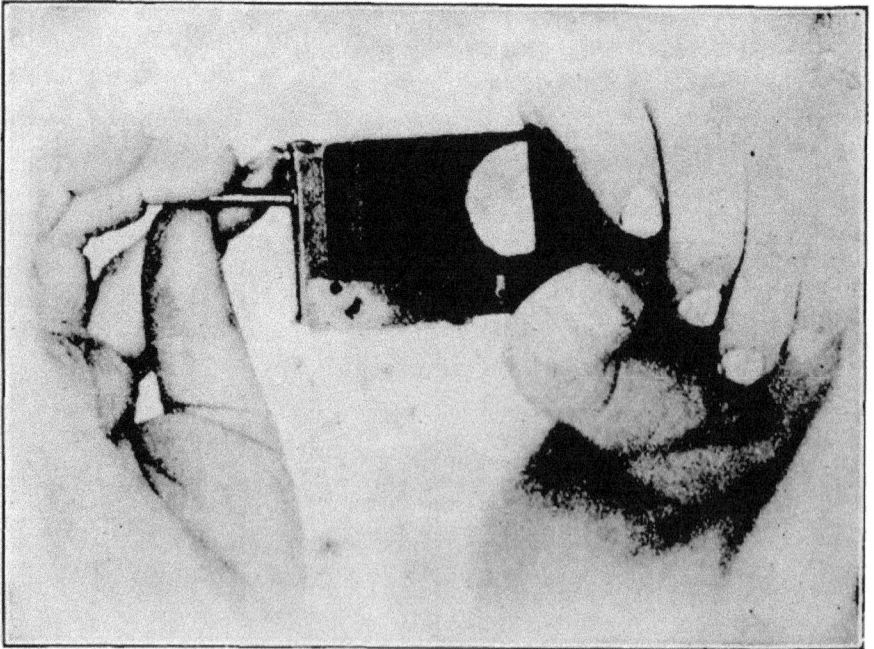

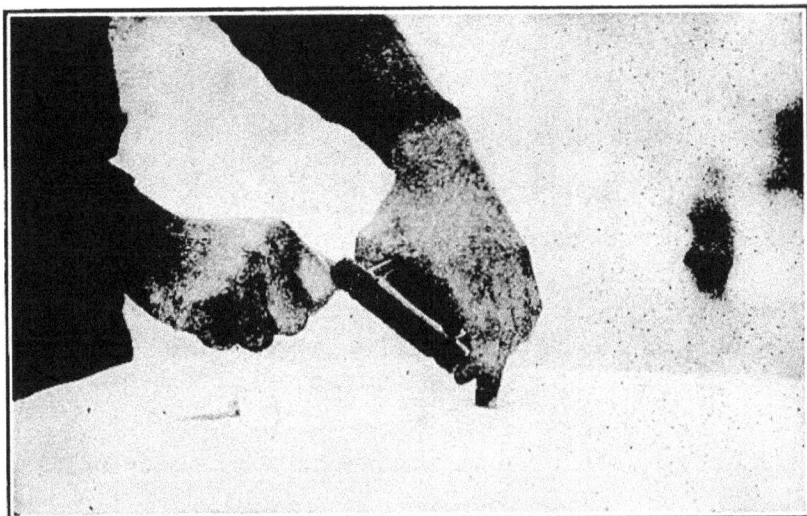

With point of a cartridge raise rear end of magazine base until indentations are clear to permit withdrawal. Then slide the base to the rear.

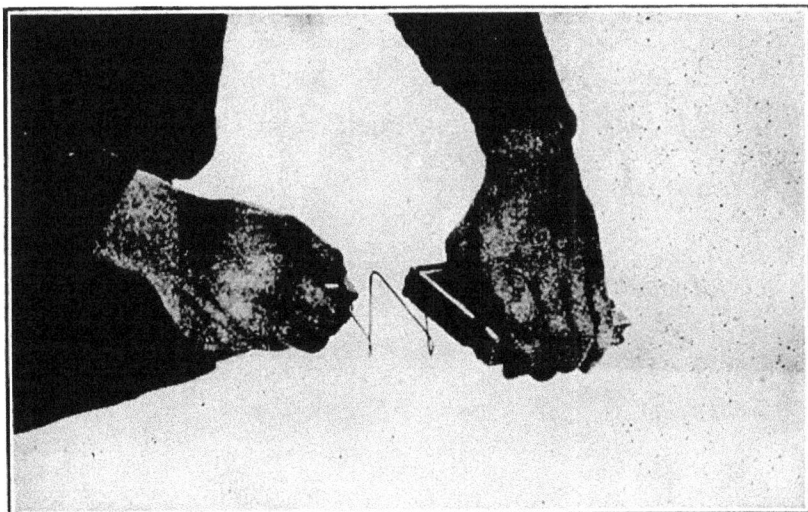

Pull out magazine spring and shake out the follower.

(For assembling): Insert follower and magazine spring.

Compress magazine spring into position.

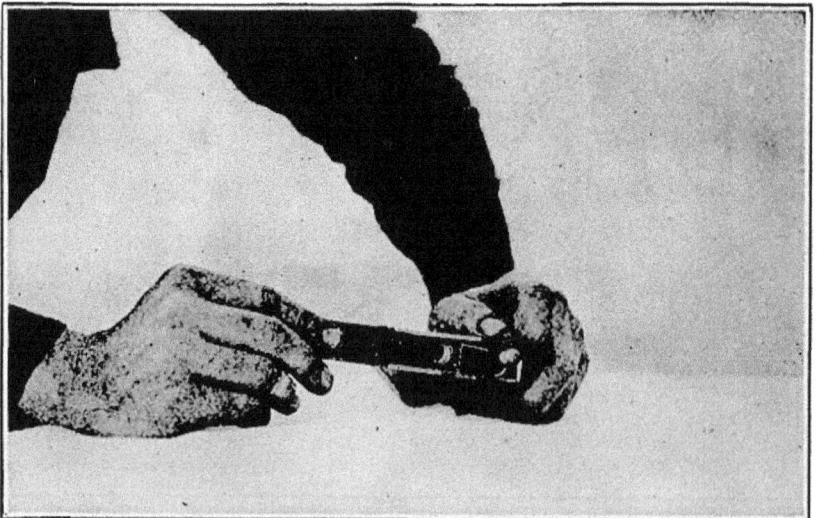

With the left hand hold the magazine spring in position.   Slide the magazine base fully home.

42

The sear is now inserted and the recoil spring guide forced through so as to register the holes in the sear, sear carrier, and trigger guard for the sear pin, and is forced in by pressing it against a wooden surface, thus forcing the recoil spring guide out.

(3) In assembling the connector, note that its head is in rear of the connector stop.

(4) Be especially careful to see that the outside prongs of the sear spring rest on their seats on the sear, and that the middle prong rides freely in the slot formed by the walls of the sear carrier. If this middle prong rests on one of these walls, instead of riding freely between them, the trigger mechanism will not function when the barrel is inclined below the horizontal.

STRIPPING AND ASSEMBLING MAGAZINE.

SEQUENCE OF STRIPPING AND ASSEMBLING.
(Not to be done in the field.)

32. (1) Magazine base.

(2) Magazine spring.

(3) Magazine follower.

To remove magazine base, raise the rear end until indentations thereon are clear, then slide to the rear. The follower and spring will then fall out.

ASSEMBLE IN REVERSE ORDER.

(1) Follower.

(2) Spring.

(3) Magazine base.

Note that the bent over end of follower and the eye of spring work against the inside of rear (notched) end of magazine.

Students must be taught that the magazine requires the same care and preservation as the rifle. It must not be allowed to become dirty. Dented magazines cause malfunctions. The greatest possible care should be taken to prevent any damage whatever being done to the lips of the magazine or to the notch for the magazine catch.

STRIPPING AND ASSEMBLING NOT ORDINARILY PERFORMED IN THE FIELD.

FOREARM GROUP.

33. To strip the forearm group, unscrew the forearm screws, long and short, and remove the wood forearm from the gas cylinder tube. The forearm escutcheon should never be removed from the forearm. Unscrew the two bracket swivel screws which allow the removal of the gun sling swivel, and the gun sling link. Spring the front swivel bracket off over the gas cylinder tube.

Before removing the gas cylinder, note its setting carefully, so that it can be reassembled to the same position. Then force out the gas cylinder lock until its head clears the notch in the gas cylinder, which can then be unscrewed from the gas cylinder tube. The gas cylinder lock can be completely removed from the cylinder with a suitable drift or by prying under the head with the combination tool.

To assemble the forearm group, replace the forearm on the gas cylinder tube, and insert the forearm screws, long and short. Spring the front swivel bracket over the gas cylinder tube, and replace the gun sling link and swivel, fastening these in place by means of the bracket swivel screws. All screws should be drawn up tight. Screw the gas cylinder in the gas cylinder tube to its proper setting, and push in the gas cylinder lock so that its head engages the notch in the gas cylinder. The registration of gas port is indicated by the circle marking on the front of the cylinder. When on the small port, the smallest circle is toward the barrel and in this position the cylinder should be about one turn from the shoulder. Unscrew one-third of a turn successively to register the larger ports.

BARREL GROUP.

34. The barrel should never be removed until replacement is necessary and then only in a properly equipped shop. Before removing the barrel, strip the receiver of the gas operating, firing, and trigger mechanism. Barrels can sometimes be unscrewed with the combination tool by engaging the spanner in the notch provided in the breech end of the barrel. A special barrel dismounting wrench for the Browning automatic rifle is provided for use in ordnance shops. This wrench should be clamped tightly around the breech end of the barrel with the handle extending to the right. The barrel can then be started by a quick downward movement of the handle. The receiver may be held in a vise or by means of a block of wood inserted up between the side walls of the receiver.

The components attached to the barrel should never be removed except when replacements are necessary or for purposes of salvaging. Unscrew the flash hider with the combination tool. Drive out the front sight carrier key pin, drive the front sight carrier off to the front, and remove the front sight carrier key. The gas cylinder tube bracket can then be driven off to the front after the pin has been driven out. These parts should be replaced in the reverse order.

When replacing a barrel always be sure that it is tight enough in the receiver never to work loose. Screw the barrel into the receiver until the draw line matches that of the receiver. Then assemble the gas cylinder tube to see if the gas cylinder tube bracket on the barrel lines up properly. If it does not, the barrel should be turned very slightly until the alignment is correct.

BUTT STOCK AND BUFFER GROUP.

35. The butt stock bolt can be unscrewed by inserting a long screw driver through the hole in the butt plate after the butt plate trap has been opened. To do this with the combination tool the butt plate must first be removed by unscrewing the butt plate screws, long and short. As soon as the butt stock bolt has been loosened the butt stock can be withdrawn to the rear. To strip the butt plate, unscrew and remove the butt plate trap spring screw and spring. Then drive out the butt plate trap axis pin and remove the butt plate trap.

The removal of the butt stock allows the stripping of the buffer mechanism. Unscrew the buffer nut and remove to the rear in the

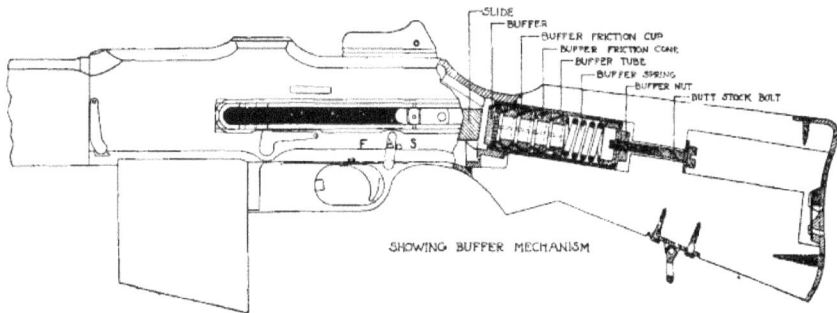

SHOWING BUFFER MECHANISM

order mentioned, the buffer spring, the four sets of buffer friction cups and cones, and the buffer. The buffer tube is threaded into the receiver, and should never be removed except for replacement. In order to assemble the butt stock and buffer mechanism, reverse the method given above.

REAR SIGHT GROUP.

36. The rear sight is to be removed or stripped only when a replacement of certain part or parts is necessary. Remove the rear sight spring screw, and drive the rear sight base out to the rear. Unscrew the rear sight axis screw and nut, and take out the rear sight leaf. The rear sight spring can then be removed from the base. Unscrew the rear sight slide stop screw which will allow the slide to be withdrawn from the leaf. With a small drift, drive out the sight slide catch axis pin and take off the slide catch and spring. To reassemble the above components reverse the order given for stripping.

37. To strip the operating handle press in on the operating handle plunger, and push out the operating handle plunger pin toward the countersunk side of the plunger. The plunger and spring can then be removed. Reverse the above method in reassembling.

The bolt guide spring may be lifted out of its seat in the bolt guide with the rim of a cartridge. The guide and spring can then be removed from the receiver. To reassemble these parts, insert the longer turned-over end of the bolt guide spring in its hole on the inside of the receiver. Then replace the bolt guide and hold it while the spring is pushed over until the shorter turned-over end engages the groove in the bolt guide. The change lever stop and spring can be removed after the change lever stop spring pin has been driven out. This is never to be done except when necessary.

FUNCTIONING.

DETAILED DESCRIPTION.

38. The rifle can best be described under two headings: The stationary portions and the moving portions.

The stationary portions consist of the receiver and parts directly or indirectly attached thereto.

The receiver (1) is made of a single piece of steel formed at the rear end to receive the butt stock (125) and the buffer tube (65), which latter part is threaded into the receiver. The butt stock is held in place by the butt stock bolt (126) which threads into the rear end of the buffer. The buffer tube contains, from front to rear, the buffer (66), four sets of buffer friction cups (68) and cones (67), the buffer spring (70), and the buffer nut (69). The bronze buffer friction cups fit over the steel cones and are split to allow expansion when under pressure. The butt plate (130) is attached to the butt stock by means of screws (136 and 137). Butt plate is provided with a trap (131) which when open will allow the removal of the butt stock bolt. The butt swivel bracket (150) is fastened to the bottom of the butt stock by means of screws (151). To this bracket is attached the gun sling swivel (148) and link (149), and the bracket swivel (143) by means of bracket swivel screws (147). This swivel arrangement provides a three-way motion for the gun sling strap connection.

The marking for the rifle is rolled on the top of the receiver at the front end. In rear of this marking the top plate (2) is fitted into dovetail guides in the receiver. The rear sight base (94) is driven into dovetail grooves at the rear end of the top of the receiver. The rear sight base is further positioned by the rear sight

LEFT SIDE VIEW OF RECEIVER

SECTION B-B

SECTION A-A

* INDICATES PIECES NOT SHOWN ON THIS DRAWING

SECTIONS
BROWNING AUTOMATIC
RIFLE
MODEL OF 1918

SUPERSEDES OLD TRACING 11144 UNDER REV. DATE OF MAR. 7, 1940

CLASS 36

DRAWING 44

1	RECEIVER
2	BOLT SUPPORT, RIGHT *
3	BOLT SUPPORT, LEFT *
4	BOLT SUPPORT RIVET
5	SLIDE
6	TRIGGER GUARD
8	TRIGGER GUARD RETAINING PIN
11	TRIGGER GUARD RETAINING PIN HANDLE
12	TRIGGER
13	TRIGGER PIN
14	CONNECTOR PIN
15	CONNECTOR
16	CONNECTOR SPRING
17	CHANGE LEVER
18	CHANGE LEVER SPRING
19	SEAR STOP
20	CHANGE LEVER STOP
21	CHANGE LEVER STOP SPRING
22	CHANGE LEVER STOP SPRING PIN
23	SEAR
25	SEAR CARRIER
26	CONNECTOR STOP
27	COUNTER RECOIL SPRING
28	EJECTOR
29	EJECTOR LOCK
30	EJECTOR SPRING
31	MAGAZINE CATCH
32	MAGAZINE CATCH SPRING
33	MAGAZINE CATCH PIN

40	RECOIL SPRING GUIDE
41	RECOIL SPRING GUIDE HEAD
42	SLIDE
43	GAS PISTON
44	GAS PISTON BUSHING
45	GAS PISTON PLUG
51	GAS CYLINDER LOCK
52	GAS CYLINDER TUBE
53	GAS CYLINDER TUBE RETAINING PIN
54	GAS CYLINDER TUBE RETAINING PIN HANDLE
56	GAS CYLINDER TUBE BRACKET
57	GAS CYLINDER TUBE BRACKET PIN
60	BARREL
61	FRONT SIGHT CARRIER
62	FRONT SIGHT CARRIER KEY
63	FRONT SIGHT CARRIER KEY PIN
64	FRONT SIGHT BLADE
66	REAR SIGHT TUBE
67	BUFFER TUBE
68	BUFFER
69	BUFFER FRICTION CONE
70	BUFFER FRICTION CUP
71	BUFFER NUT
73	BOLT GUIDE
74	BOLT GUIDE LOCK
75	BOLT GUIDE SPRING
76	FIRING PIN
78	EXTRACTOR
79	EXTRACTOR SPRING

80	BOLT LOCK
81	BOLT LOCK PIN
82	LINK
83	LINK PIN
85	HAMMER
86	HAMMER PIN
87	OPERATING HANDLE
88	OPERATING HANDLE PLUNGER
89	OPERATING HANDLE PLUNGER PIN
90	OPERATING HANDLE PLUNGER SPRING
92	REAR SIGHT BASE
93	REAR SIGHT SPRING
95	REAR SIGHT AXIS SCREW
96	REAR SIGHT AXIS SCREW NUT
97	REAR SIGHT SLIDE
98	REAR SIGHT SLIDE CATCH
99	REAR SIGHT SLIDE CATCH SPRING *
100	REAR SIGHT SLIDE STOP SCREW
101	REAR SIGHT LEAF
102	MAGAZINE
103	MAGAZINE BASE
104	MAGAZINE FOLLOWER
105	MAGAZINE FILLER
108	COMBINATION TOOL
115	FOREARM SCREW - SHORT
119	FOREARM SCREW - LONG
120	FOREARM ESCUTCHEON

128	BUTT STOCK
129	BUTT STOCK BOLT
130	BUTT STOCK BOLT WASHER
131	BUTT PLATE
132	BUTT PLATE TRAP
133	BUTT PLATE TRAP SPRING
134	BUTT PLATE TRAP AXIS PIN
135	BUTT PLATE TRAP SPRING SCREW
136	BUTT PLATE SCREW, LONG
137	BUTT PLATE SCREW, SHORT
140	GUN SLING HOOK
141	GUN SLING SLIDE CATCH
142	GUN SLING SLIDE CATCH SPRING
143	BRACKET, SWIVEL
145	FRONT SWIVEL BRACKET
146	BRACKET SWIVEL SCREW
147	GUN SLING SWIVEL
149	BUTT SWIVEL BRACKET
150	BUTT SWIVEL BRACKET SCREW
151	GAS PISTON RETAINING PIN A
152	GAS CYLINDER TUBE RETAINING PIN KEY *
148	GUN SLING HOOK RIVETS
151	GUN SLING STRAP - LONG
152	GUN SLING STRAP - SHORT

47

spring screw (96). The rear sight leaf (104) is pivoted at the rear of the rear sight base, its operation being controlled by the rear sight spring (95). The rear sight slide (99) and slide catch (100) operate up and down on the rear sight leaf in such a way as to give a range adjustment of from 100 to 1,600 yards. The leaf is also provided with a battle sight.

The ejection opening is located on the right side of the receiver, as is the hammer pin hole. The hammer pin hole is located so as to allow the disassembling of the hammer pin and subsequent parts.

The left side of the receiver is provided with a guide for the operating handle (88). The operating handle is fitted with a plunger (89) which is held in place by a pin (90), and which is operated by a spring (91) in such a way as to retain the operating handle in the forward position unless force is applied to move it toward the rear. The bolt guide (72) is held in the side of the receiver above the operating handle by the bolt guide spring (73), which is attached to the inside of the receiver. The edge of the bolt guide projects inside the receiver forming a support for the bolt (75) when it is in the rear position. The change lever stop (20) is also assembled to the left side of the receiver, this part being held in place by the change lever stop spring (21), which is pinned to the inside of the receiver.

The bolt supports, right (3) and left (4), are riveted to the inside of the receiver by means of three bolt support rivets (5) each, in such a way as to support the bolt (75) when it is in its forward position. The rear corners of the bolt supports are rounded so as to aid by their camming action the raising of the bolt lock (80). The inner edges of the bolt supports are formed to guide the cartridge into the chamber as it is stripped from the magazine. The locking shoulder of the receiver is located just in rear of the top plate. This shoulder supports the bolt lock and bolt when the cartridge is fired.

The bottom of the receiver is left open to receive the magazine at the front end. The rear portion of the opening is closed by the trigger guard (10), which fits up between the sides of the receiver. The rear end of the trigger guard is supported by a tongue in the receiver, which fits into a corresponding groove in the trigger guard. The forward end of the trigger guard is held in place by the trigger guard retaining pin (11). The trigger guard retaining pin handle (12) locks in an indentation in the receiver, thus holding the pin in place.

The ejector (29) is retained in a **T** cut at the front end of the trigger guard by means of the ejector lock (30) and spring (31). The top of the ejector extends upward in such a way as to operate in the ejector cut in the bolt. The magazine catch (32) is pinned to the trigger guard. The upper end projects through the ejector, and provides a catch which holds the magazine in place. The magazine catch spring (33) is positioned between the ejector and the magazine catch, below the pivot point of the latter. This holds the upper end of the magazine catch in the forward position. The magazine release extends forward from the trigger guard and operates against the lower end of the magazine catch, thus moving the upper end of the catch rearward when the release is pushed forward.

The trigger (13) is pivoted to the trigger guard by the trigger pin (14). The connector (16) fits loosely in the trigger, the lower notch riding on the connector pin (15). The upper edge of the connector comes in contact with the front end of the sear (23) when the trigger is raised. The cam surface in rear of this edge engages the corresponding surface of the sear carrier (25) if the change lever (17) has been set at "F." The sear (23) is pivoted near the rear end of the trigger guard by the sear pin (24) which passes through the trigger guard and the sear carrier (25), the holes in the trigger guard being slotted. The rear end of the sear is provided with a nose which engages the sear notch in the slide (45). The under surface of the front end of the sear engages the connector when it is raised by the action of the trigger. The sear spring (26) is held in grooves in the trigger guard. This spring is of the leaf type, the middle tongue bearing against the connector holding this latter part in position. The two outside tongues of the sear spring bear downward against the forward end of the sear.

The change lever (17) extends laterally through the trigger guard, being held in place by the front tongue of the change-lever spring (18). This tongue also engages in notches around the shaft of the change lever, thus holding the change lever in the various positions. The handle of the change lever extends upward along the left side of the receiver on which is marked the positions: " F " for semiautomatic fire, "A" for full automatic fire, and " S " for safety. The cuts and lugs on the under side of the change-lever shaft control the action of the trigger and connector, thus giving the classes of fire mentioned. The change-lever stop (20) in the receiver prevents the change lever from being set at safety without intention. The change-lever spring (18) is held in the trigger guard by means of grooves. The sear stop (19) is assembled to the rear tongue of this spring. The sear carrier (25) is held in place at the rear end by the sear pin and at the front end by the trigger pin, the holes in the sear carrier for the trigger pin being slotted so as to allow a certain amount of movement of the sear carrier in a forward direction. This movement is arrested by the counter-recoil spring (28)

which surrounds the spindle at the front end of the sear carrier,
bearing against the front shoulder of the sear carrier and the opposite shoulder of the trigger guard. Thus, when a shock is imposed
upon the sear it is transmitted to the sear carrier through the sear
pin, which operates in slotted holes in the trigger guard. The
trigger operates between the side walls of the sear carrier. The
connector stop (27) is in the form of a pin passing between these
side walls and forming a stop which prevents excessive forward
movement of the connector.

The forward end of the receiver near the top is threaded to receive
the barrel (60) which is screwed in tightly to the draw marks. The
barrel is of plain, light construction, the large diameter at the breech
end being carried well forward of the chamber. The chambering
and rifling of the barrel are of the usual design for U. S. caliber
.30, model 1906, ammunition. The gas port is provided on the
under side of the barrel about 6 inches from the muzzle end. This
port corresponds to a similar port in the gas cylinder tube bracket
(56) which surrounds the barrel at this point, being held in place
by the gas cylinder bracket pin (57). The gas port extends
through this bracket, which is provided with a T cut which re-
tains the front end of the gas cylinder tube (52). The front-sight
carrier (61) surrounds the muzzle end of the barrel. This carrier
is held in place by the front-sight carrier key (62) and the front-
sight carrier key pin (63). The front-sight blade (64), which is
of the usual construction, dovetails transversely into the top of the
front-sight carrier. The front-sight blades vary in height in ac-
cordance with the requirements of targeting the rifle at the factory.
After targeting, the blade is staked in place with a prick punch.
The muzzle end of the barrel is threaded to receive the flash hider
(154), which is of plain, tubular construction, provided with a hole
at the rear end, which takes the combination tool.

The rear end of the gas cylinder tube (52) is held up into the receiver by the gas cylinder tube retaining pin (53), the handle of
which locks in an indentation in the left side of the receiver. The
tube provides a guide way for the gas piston (46), and is threaded
at the front end to receive the gas cylinder (50). This end is notched
to engage the gas cylinder lock (51). The ribs at the top engage the
T cut in the bracket of the barrel holding the gas ports in close contact. The shoulder at the rear end of the tube provides a stop for the
front end of the slide (45). The lugs above this bear against the
barrel. The rear portion of the barrel and gas cylinder tube are protected on the bottom and sides by a large wooden forearm (118),
which is attached to the gas cylinder tube by means of the forearm
screws, long (120) and short (119). The forearm escutcheon (131)

is permanently seated in the forearm, and acts as a nut for the fore-arm screw, long. The outside of the forearm is cut to provide a good gripping surface for the hand.

The recoil spring guide head (42) engages retaining shoulders in the front end of the receiver. The rear surface of this head is checkered to facilitate stripping and assembling. The recoil spring guide (41) is riveted into the head which forms the rear seat for the recoil spring (40). The rear portion of this spring is guided by the recoil spring guide, the front portion being retained in the hollow gas piston (46).

The front swivel bracket (145) clamps around the gas cylinder tube in front of the forearm. The gun sling swivel and link (148–149) and the bracket swivel (143) are attached to the front swivel bracket by bracket swivel screws (147) in the manner described for the butt swivel bracket.

The gas cylinder lock (51) fits in the transverse hole through the head of the gas cylinder (50). The cylinder is provided with three gas ports of varying size. These are located around the circumfer-ence of the cylinder wall, the position and size of each being indi-cated by circles marked on the cylinder head. The notches for the head of the gas cylinder lock are located so as to register the gas port in the cylinder, indicated by the circle marking nearest the barrel. The inside of the gas cylinder is recessed at the forward end to pro-vide clearance for dirt and powder fouling.

39. The moving portions consist of the operating, breech, and firing mechanisms.

The rings at the front of the gas piston (46) operate in the gas cylinder. The rear end of the piston threads loosely into the front end of the slide (45), and is held from rotation by the gas piston retaining pin (49). The piston is of hollow construction, the front end being closed by the gas piston plug (48) and a bearing for the forward end of the recoil spring being provided by the gas piston bushing (47).

The slide (45) extends rearward in longitudinal grooves in the re-ceiver, clearance for the magazine being provided between the sides of the slide. The rear end of the slide is beveled slightly to form a parallel line of contact against the buffer. A sear notch is cut in the under side of the slide. The hammer (85) is held in the guides in the slide by the hammer pin (86), which also acts as the lower pivot for the link (82). After the breech has locked, the front face of the hammer strikes the firing pin. The link is pinned to the bolt lock (80) by the link pin (83). The upper and rearward projection of the link forms a bearing surface against which the bolt lock rests during the recoiling movement. This holds the rear end of the bolt lock up.

The rear locking surface of the bolt lock (80) bears against the corresponding surface of the receiver as the cartridge is ignited. The under side of the bolt lock is slotted, and a cam surface provided which engages the retracting cam of the firing pin (76). The front end of the bolt lock bears against the bolt (75) with which it is permanently hinged by means of the bolt lock pin (81). The bolt carries the firing pin (76), the retracting cam of the latter operating in the slot in the rear tail, or firing pin guide, of the bolt. The head of the firing pin extends rearward from this guide, and when struck by the hammer causes the firing pin point to project through the hole in the front face of the bolt, thus igniting the cartridge, the base of which is supported by the face of the bolt. The extractor (77) and extractor spring (78) are positioned in a recess at the front end of the bolt so that the extractor will engage the rim of the cartridge as it is driven forward into the chamber. A lug on the extractor engages a groove in the recess in the bolt and prevents the extractor from pulling out to the front.

40. The magazine consists of four pieces: the magazine tube (108), base (109), follower (110), and spring (111). The magazine tube is formed to receive a staggered double row of cartridges. Magazines having a capacity of 20 rounds are issued to rifle companies, a 40-round magazine being used especially for antiaircraft fire. A notch is cut in the rear edge of the tube which engages the magazine catch. The upper lips of the tube are formed to facilitate feeding. The magazine follower operates upward against the cartridges under the action of the magazine spring, which is supported at the bottom by the magazine base. The construction of 40-round magazines is similar to the 20-round type, except the tube is deeper and is fitted with two springs separated by a spacer.

BRIEF OF ACTION.

41. The functioning of the Browning automatic rifle is divided into two phases based on the natural operation of the mechanism when a shot is fired. These two phases are the backward action (first phase) and the forward action (second phase). In making this division the ignition of the cartridge in the chamber is assumed as a starting or reference point.

First phase:
    (1) Action of gas.
    (2) Slide.
    (3) Unlocking.
    (4) Withdrawal of firing pin.
    (5) Extraction.
    (6) Ejection.

(7) Termination of first phase.

Second phase:

(1) Action of recoil spring.

(2) Feeding.

(3) Locking.

(4) Ignition.

(5) Termination of second phase.

DETAILED FUNCTIONING.

42. The instructor will give a brief lecture explaining the difference between recoil-operated and gas-operated rifles, and that all automatic weapons must have mechanical means for performing the following functions: Extraction, ejection, feeding, locking the breech while there is a high pressure in the bore, and igniting the cartridge. He will define and illustrate any mechanical terms which he uses; for instance, "to cam" is to change the direction of motion of a part by means of sliding contact between two surfaces. Instructor may illustrate this by showing how the bolt supports act on the bolt lock during the operation of unlocking.

The operations of extraction, ejection, etc., are performed by various cams, lugs, and springs, and the energy necessary to perform this work and to overcome friction in the rifle is derived from the explosion of the powder in the chamber.

He will explain that these operations have a certain sequence in various rifles and that some of them are concurrent, and that with the Browning automatic rifle students will be expected to learn and understand thoroughly the various operations separately, and then to visualize them as they actually occur in the rifle during firing.

EXPLANATORY DEMONSTRATION.

43. This explanatory demonstration will be illustrated with an assembled rifle, parts of rifles, drawing and sectional views, together with motion pictures and wooden models of the trigger mechanism and the bolt, wherever possible to obtain them.

It is not desired to have the soldier memorize the distances given below. He must have, however, an approximate idea of these distances; for example, he should understand that the backward travel of the bolt has been very little when the bolt lock is drawn completely down, but that, on the other hand, the slide has moved a considerable distance.

FIRST PHASE.

ACTION OF GAS.

44. A cartridge having been ignited, the bullet, under the pressure of the expanding powder gases, travels through the barrel, and when it reaches a point 6 inches from the muzzle, it passes a port in the bottom of the barrel. The barrel pressure, which at this instant is still very high, seeks this first natural vent. Registered with the barrel port are other similar ports in the gas cylinder tube bracket, gas cylinder tube and gas cylinder. The port in the gas cylinder is the smallest and serves to throttle the barrel pressure. The ports in the gas cylinder lead radially into a well about one-eighth of an inch in diameter in the head of the gas cylinder. The throttled barrel pressure is conducted through this well to the gas piston plug. This pressure acts on the piston a very short time, namely, the time it takes the bullet to travel the 6-inch distance from the barrel port to the

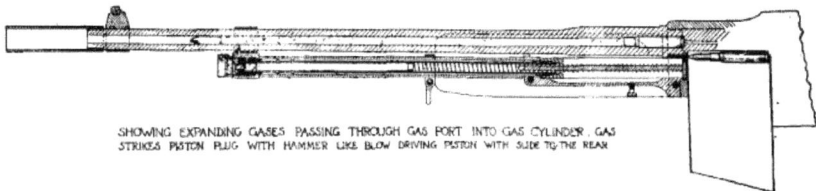

SHOWING EXPANDING GASES PASSING THROUGH GAS PORT INTO GAS CYLINDER. GAS STRIKES PISTON PLUG WITH HAMMER LIKE BLOW DRIVING PISTON WITH SLIDE TO THE REAR

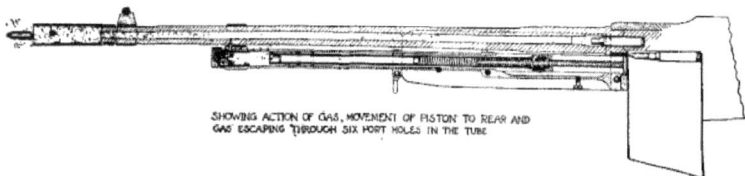

SHOWING ACTION OF GAS, MOVEMENT OF PISTON TO REAR AND GAS ESCAPING THROUGH SIX PORT HOLES IN THE TUBE

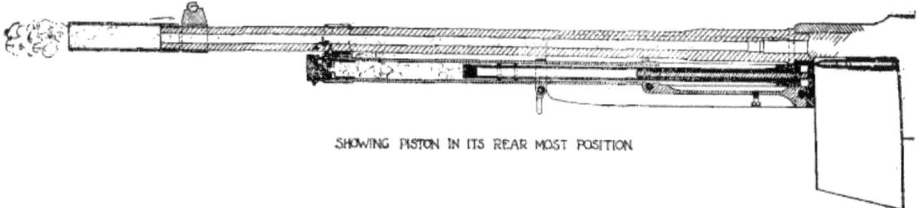

SHOWING PISTON IN ITS REAR MOST POSITION

muzzle. Its effect is that of a sudden, severe blow on the piston plug. Under the influence of this blow the gas piston is driven to the rear and carries with it the slide to which it is assembled. When the piston has traveled about nine-sixteenths of an inch backward, the bearing rings on its head, also the gas piston plug, pass out of the cylinder. The gas expands around the piston head and into the gas cylinder tube, and is exhausted through 6 portholes in the tube, just in rear of the gas cylinder tube bracket. The gas is prevented in a large measure from traveling back through the gas cylinder tube by two rings on the piston, about five-eighths of an inch apart and $1\frac{1}{4}$ inches from the piston head. These rings also serve as bearings to hold the front end of the piston in the center of the gas cylinder tube after the piston head has passed out of the gas cylinder.

Having traced out the action of the gas, the action of the mechanism as it moves to the rear will be considered. The first and immediate result of the backward movement of the slide is the beginning of the compression of the recoil spring, thereby storing energy for the forward action.

UNLOCKING.

The hammer pin is slightly in advance of the link pin. about 0.19 of an inch. The center rib of the hammer is very slightly in rear of the head of the firing pin. When the slide begins its motion to the rear it imparts no motion whatever to the bolt and bolt lock. The slide moves back 0.19 of an inch and its only effect during this travel is to carry the hammer from the firing pin and the hammer pin directly under the link pin. At this point the unlocking begins. the link revolves forward about the hammer pin, drawing the bolt lock down and to the rear. The motion of the lock and bolt, which is zero at the instant the hammer pin passes under the link pin, accelerates from this point until the slide has traveled about 1.2 inches, at which point the lock is drawn completely down out of the locking recess and away from the locking shoulder of the receiver. It is now supported in front of the bolt supports, and the front upper shoulder of the link has revolved forward and bears upon the locking shoulder of the bolt lock. These two influences prevent the bolt lock from revolving down below the line of backward travel of the bolt.

WITHDRAWAL OF FIRING PIN.

As the bolt lock revolves down from its locked position, a cam surface in a slot in the rear bottom side of the bolt lock comes in contact with a similar cam surface on the firing pin lug, and cams the firing pin from the face of the bolt.

EXTRACTION.

The backward motion of the bolt begins when the bolt lock has been drawn down so that the circular cam surface on its under side is operating on the rear shoulders of the bolt supports. This produces a strong lever action which slowly loosens the cartridge case. The backward travel of the bolt has been slight, only about five thirty-seconds of an inch when the firing pin is withdrawn; its travel is about eleven thirty-seconds of an inch when the bolt lock is completely drawn down. From this point the bolt moves to the rear, drawn by the bolt lock and link, with the same speed as the slide, and carries with it the empty cartridge case, which is held firmly in its seat on the face of the bolt by the extractor. The extractor is on the upper right-hand side of the bolt next to the ejection opening in the receiver. A slot cut in the left side of the bolt lock near the back end passes over the bolt guide, which supports the bolt lock and bolt when they are in the rear position.

EJECTION.

When the slide reaches a point about one-quarter of an inch from the end of its travel, the base of the cartridge case strikes the ejector, which is on the left side of the feed rib of the bolt, and opposite the extractor. This action causes the cartridge case to be pivoted with considerable force about the extractor, and through the ejection opening in the receiver. The front end of the cartridge case passes first out of the receiver, and is pivoted so that it strikes the outside of the receiver at a point about 1 inch in rear of the ejection opening. It rebounds from the receiver toward the right front.

TERMINATION OF FIRST PHASE.

The backward motion is terminated when the rear end of the slide strikes the buffer. The slide moves forward one-tenth of an inch, after striking the buffer, under the action of the recoil spring, but if the sear nose is not depressed, it engages the sear notch on the slide, and the piece is cocked for the next shot.

NOTE.—It is to be noted that the motion of the bolt, bolt lock, and link mechanism began slowly at first and did not attain the speed of the slide until the latter had traveled about $1\frac{1}{4}$ inches backward. This is a very important characteristic of the rifle, since on this account the mechanism is not subjected to an excess strain due to a sudden start at the instant the gas impinges upon the piston. This slow start delays the opening of the chamber sufficiently to allow the high barrel pressure to decrease.

SECOND PHASE.

ACTION OF RECOIL SPRING.

45. The sear nose is depressed, disengaging the sear, and the slide moves forward under the action of the recoil spring. The position of the link pin is slightly below a line joining the bolt lock pin and the hammer pin; therefore as the slide starts forward the joint at the link pin has a tendency to buckle downward. It is prevented from doing this by the tail of the feed rib on the bolt which extends backward under the bolt lock, also by the upper front shoulder of the link being in contact with the locking surface of the bolt lock. Since the joint can not buckle, the entire mechanism moves forward with the slide. When it has traveled about one-quarter of an inch the front end of the feed rib impinges on the base of the top cartridge, which the magazine spring and lips are holding up in its path.

FEEDING.

The cartridge is carried forward about one-quarter of an inch, when the nose of the bullet strikes the bullet ramp or guide on the breech of barrel, and is deflected upward toward the chamber. This action also guides the front end of the cartridge from under the magazine lips. The base of the cartridge approaches the center of the magazine, where the lips are cut away and the opening enlarged, and at this point is forced out of the magazine by the magazine spring. The base of the cartridge slides across the face of the bolt and under the extractor. Should the cartridge fail to slide under the extractor, the extractor will snap over its head as the bolt reaches the forward position. When the cartridge is released by the magazine, the nose of the bullet is so far in the chamber that it is guided by the chamber from this point on.

LOCKING.

When the slide is about 2 inches from its forward position the circular cam surface on the under side of the bolt lock begins to ride over the rear shoulders of the bolt supports, and the rear end of the bolt lock is cammed upward. The link pin passes up above the line joining the bolt lock pin and hammer pin. The joint at the link pin now has a tendency to buckle upward, and the bolt lock being opposite the locking recess in the receiver, is free to, and does, pivot upward about the bolt lock pin. The link revolves upward about the hammer pin, forcing the bolt lock up, and a rounded surface on the bolt lock just above the locking face slips over the locking shoulder in the receiver, giving the lock a lever action which forces the bolt home to its final position. The two locking surfaces on the bolt lock and the receiver register as the hammer pin passes under the link pin.

IGNITING THE CARTRIDGE.

The lug on the firing pin is buried in the slot on the under side of the bolt lock at all times except when the bolt is locked in the forward position. Therefore, the firing pin is locked away from the face of the bolt during all the backward and forward motion of the bolt. When the hammer pin passes under the link pin, the firing pin has been released by the bolt lock. The slide and hammer move forward about one-tenth of an inch farther, and the center rib of the hammer strikes the head of the firing pin, driving it forward, and igniting the cartridge.

TERMINATION OF SECOND PHASE.

The forward end of the slide strikes a shoulder at the rear end of the gas cylinder tube which terminates the forward motion. The forward motion is not terminated by the hammer on the firing pin. This can be seen by examining the head of the firing pin when the gas cylinder tube is assembled to the receiver, and the bolt mechanism is in the forward position. The firing pin has still about one-sixteenth of an inch clearance from its extreme forward position.

NOTE.—The locking shoulder of the receiver is inclined forward. Its surface is perpendicular to the line through the bolt lock which the shock of the explosion follows; therefore, the force of this shock is exerted squarely against this normal surface. It should be noted that the speed of the bolt mechanism is slowed down gradually from the instant that the bolt lock starts to rise until the hammer pin passes under the link pin, when its speed is zero.

FUNCTIONING OF BUFFER.

46. The buffer system consists of a tube, in which are placed successively from front to rear, the buffer head; a brass friction cup with concave interior which is split to allow for expansion; a steel cone to fit into the cup; four of these cups and cones are placed one after the other in series. In rear of these is the buffer spring, and finally the buffer nut, which is screwed into the end of the tube and forms a seat for the spring.

THE ACTION.

The buffer head, struck by the rear end of the slide, moves to the rear, forcing the cups over the cones and causing them to expand tightly against the tube, consequently producing considerable friction as the cups move back and compress the buffer spring. Thus the rearward motion of slide is checked gradually and there is practically no rebound. The spring returns the buffer head and friction cups and cones to their original positions.

FUNCTIONING OF TRIGGER MECHANISM.

47. The trigger mechanism has three settings: (1) Automatic (A). When so set the sear is depressed as long as the trigger is held back and the piece will continue firing until the magazine is emptied. (2) Semiautomatic (F). When so set the sear is depressed, thereby disengaging the sear and sear notch when the trigger is pulled, but the mechanism is so constructed that the sear rises and engages in the sear notch when the slide comes back again, and the sear and sear notch will not disengage until the trigger is fully released and then pulled. With this setting the piece fires one shot for each pull and

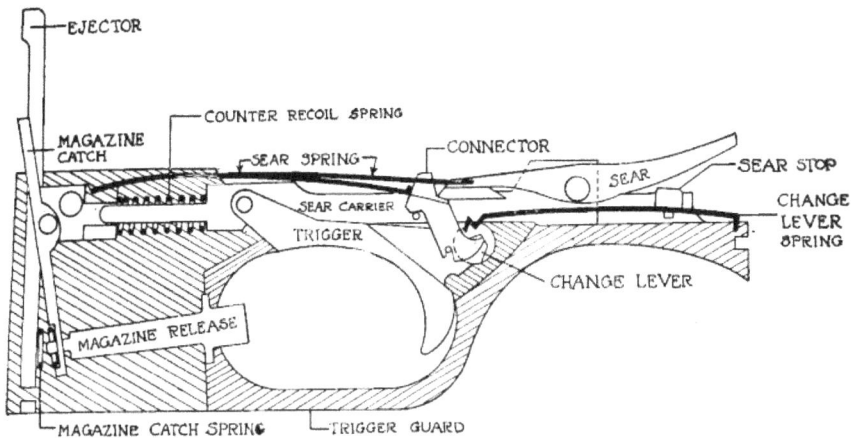

SHOWING TRIGGER MECHANISM SINGLE SHOT FIRING. THE CONNECTOR CAMMED FORWARD FROM UNDER THE FORWARD END OF THE SEAR BY THE UNDER CAM SURFACE OF THE SEAR CARRIER, PERMITS THE FORWARD END OF THE SEAR TO RETURN TO POSITION UNDER TENSION OF SEAR SPRING, CAUSING THE REAR END OF THE SEAR TO ENGAGE IN THE SEAR NOTCH IN THE SIDE.

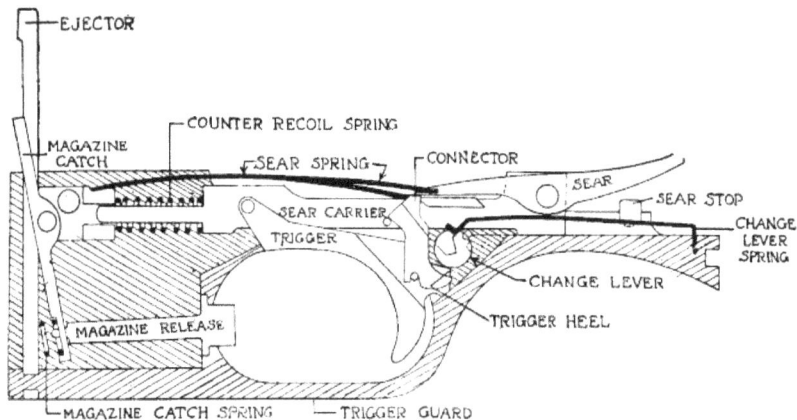

SHOWING TRIGGER MECHANISM SET ON SAFE. CYLINDRICAL PORTION OF THE CHANGE LEVER RESTING OVER THE HEEL OF THE TRIGGER PREVENTS THE UPWARD MOVEMENT OF THE TRIGGER AND THE RELEASING OF THE SEAR.

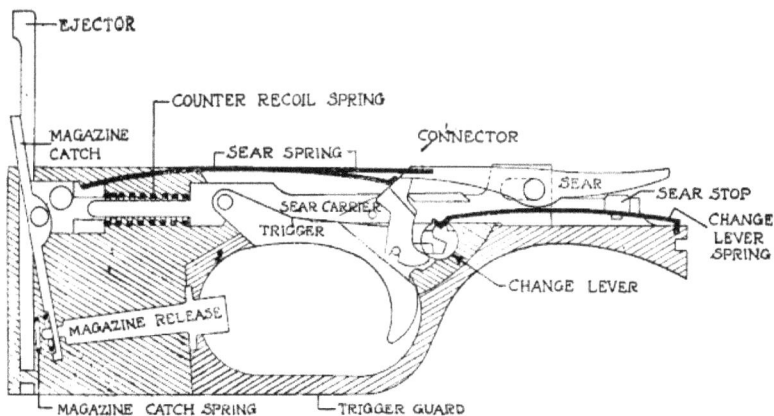

SHOWING TRIGGER MECHANISM AUTOMATIC FIRING. TOE OF THE CONNECTOR ENGAGES UNDER THE CONNECTOR STUD ON THE CHANGE LEVER, PREVENTING THE CONNECTOR FROM RISING SUFFICIENTLY HIGH TO BE CAMMED FORWARD FROM UNDER THE FORE END OF THE SEAR: HEAD OF THE CONNECTOR HOLDING UP FORE END OF SEAR, DEPRESSING REAR, PREVENTING THE REAR END OF SEAR FROM ENGAGING IN THE SEAR NOTCH OF THE SLIDE.

release of the trigger. (3) Safe (S). When so set the sear can not be released from the sear notch by pulling the trigger.

The action of the trigger mechanism is taken up in phases, and should be followed on the mechanism itself as the explanation proceeds. Have the trigger guard stripped completely. Study the shape of the change lever and note the following: (1) It is a bar about one-quarter of an inch in diameter. (2) It has three shallow longitudinal slots cut on top of the bar, as the handle is held vertically. (3) The side of the bar is slotted in such a way as to leave a little tongue of metal in the center and at the lower edge of the slot.

SETTING CHANGE LEVER.

Assemble the change lever and spring to the trigger guard. Note that the toe of the change lever spring is seated in one of the longitudinal slots on the change lever, and that as the lever is turned from one position to another it seats in the other slots. The only function of the spring and the longitudinal slots is to hold the change lever in the position in which it is set.

Assemble the trigger and pin to the guard.

Turn the change lever to rear or safe position. Note that in this position the slot is turned slightly upward, and that the full surface of the bar is on the bottom. Pull the trigger. Note that the rear top end of the trigger is slotted longitudinally, and that the metal on each side of the slot forms two shoulders which rise against the bottom of the change lever bar.

Push the change lever over to the vertical position, which is the automatic setting. Pull the trigger as before and note that the slot in the change lever is turned to the front, and that the two shoulders of the trigger, which before engaged the full surface of the change lever bar, now are free to pass up into the slot of the change lever; also that the tongue of metal on the bottom of the change lever slot passes through the longitudinal slot in the end of the trigger.

Now push change lever forward to single shot position.

Note that now the slot is turned partially down and that when the trigger is pulled the rear end of the trigger passes up into the change lever slot; also that the tongue of metal in the bottom of the change lever slot is now turned back and does not pass through the slot in the end of the trigger as it did in the automatic position.

Now observe the shape of the connector. It is shaped like a boot with a toe and heel. It has a flat surface that slopes down and toward the front from the head. (Sear spring ramp.) In rear of the head the profile extends straight downward for about one-eighth of an inch, then slopes slightly to the rear for 0.12 of an inch. (Sear carrier ramp.) This last slope is used in a cam action to be explained later. Note the narrow, flat top surface of connector. Its function is to raise the forward end of sear until cammed out from under the latter.

Place the connector on the connector pin and set change lever to safe, pull the trigger, and note that the connector is not raised, for the obvious reason that the trigger itself can not be raised because the change lever bar is in its way.

Turn change lever to automatic position, pull the trigger, and note that the head of the connector is raised and held in a vertical position and can not be tipped forward. The tongue on the change lever engages the toe of the connector as the trigger is pulled and holds the connector upright.

Turn the change lever to single shot position, pull the trigger, and note that the tongue on the change lever does not now engage the toe of the connector, and that the head of the connector can now be tipped forward.

Observe now the cross pin on the sear carrier called the connector stop; also that just in rear of the connector stop and on the under side of the sear carrier is an inclined surface sloping upward in the metal which joins the two sides of the sear carrier. This surface has a cam action with the above-mentioned surface on the connector.

Completely assemble the trigger mechanism.

Note that the center leaf of the sear spring presses on the front sloping surface of the connector and tends to press the head of the connector backward. Set change lever on safe and pull trigger. Note the head of connector is not raised above the sear carrier, for reasons given previously. Therefore, the sear nose is not depressed and hence the safe position. Change over to the automatic position and pull the trigger; the head of the connector is raised and held in the vertical position, thus depressing the sear nose and holding it in this position, which obviously gives automatic fire as long as there are cartridges in the magazine. The tongue on change lever tends to hold connector vertically and the ramp on sear carrier tends to cam connector forward. The forces exerted by these two parts on connector are opposed, hence trigger mechanism is locked when trigger has been pulled enough to release slide.

Set change lever for single shot, pull trigger slowly. Note that at first the head of the connector rises and thereby depresses the sear nose, which allows the slide to go forward. If the squeeze of the trigger is continued the previously mentioned cam surface on the connector comes in contact with the cam surface of the sear carrier, and the head of the connector is cammed forward against the pressure of the center leaf of the sear spring. The connector disengages the front arm of the sear and the two outside leaves of the sear spring depress it, and the sear nose is thereby raised up in the path of the slide and engages the sear notch when the slide moves back, thus allowing only one shot to be fired. When the trigger is released the center leaf of the sear spring presses the head of the connector downward and back under the forward end of the sear, so that when the trigger is pulled again the action is repeated and single shot is fired.

In the semiautomatic position the connector stop prevents the head of the connector being tipped so far forward that the sear spring can not push it back in place when the trigger is released. The only function of the change lever in the semiautomatic position is the limiting of the upward travel of the trigger when its upper rear shoulders strike the top of the slot in the change lever, which in this position is turned down.

METHOD OF OPERATION.

FILLING THE MAGAZINE.

48. Place the wide end of the magazine filler over the top of the magazine so that the groove in the magazine filler fits over the catch rib of the magazine. Hold the magazine in the same relative position that it occupies in the rifle; that is, with the catch rib toward the operator. Then insert a clip of cartridges in the guides provided in the filler, and with the right thumb near the base, strip the cartridges into the magazine, guiding the bullet ends if necessary with the left hand. Each magazine will hold four clips. Filling exercise will be conducted with dummy ammunition. Students should become proficient in this work.

INSERTING THE MAGAZINE.

49. The empty magazine may be withdrawn after pressing the magazine release. Hold the loaded magazine with the base in the palm of the right hand, cartridges pointing to the front. Insert the magazine between the sides of the receiver in front of the trigger guard, and push it home with the right hand. The magazine can be inserted with the mechanism in either the cocked or forward position. It is, however, ordinarily inserted after the rifle has been cocked.

SETTING THE CHANGE LEVER.

50. For semiautomatic fire, or single shot, push the change lever to the forward position, marked " F."

For full automatic fire or continuous fire to the capacity of the magazine, set the change lever in the vertical position against the change lever stop, marked " A."

To set the rifle at safe, depress the change-lever stop and pull the change lever rearward until it covers the change-lever stop. This position is marked "S."

It will be noted that the change-lever stop prevents the accidental setting of the change lever at safe, and at the same time allows a quick change from safe to either full automatic or semiautomatic fire.

USE OF SPARE PARTS AND ACCESSORIES.

51. The nomenclature of the spare parts kit will be taught according to the principles hereinbefore enunciated. This instruction will include the proper method of packing the spare parts kit. It will also include instruction in the contents of the gun box. The men should be made thoroughly familiar with the proper use of the tools and accessories provided.

SPARE PARTS.

52. The importance of knowing what is, and what is not, carried as a spare part should be impressed on all automatic riflemen.

It is essential to know where to find any spare part that may be required.

All spare parts must be given their proper names; the use of other names is forbidden.

A list of deficiencies should be kept inside each gun box.

Spare parts must be kept lightly oiled.

The necessity of checking spare parts whenever opportunity offers must be emphasized.

Breakages and losses must be reported immediately.

Noncommissioned instructors will check their own spare parts at the beginning and end of the instruction and will render a report showing deficiencies.

Worn or defective parts should not be kept in the spare parts box.

Where any rifles are kept in reserve, care should be taken to see that they are in the same condition of readiness for action as those to be used in the firing line. They should not be utilized as a source for obtaining spare parts.

SPARE PARTS CASE AND FABRIC CONTAINERS.

53. The spare parts case should be given the same care as other leather equipment. The contents should always be properly packed. The small fabric container is used to hold the recoil spring after it has been coiled up. The remaining spare parts are packed in the large fabric container.

OIL CAN AND THONG CLEANER.

54. Care should be taken to avoid denting or otherwise damaging the oil can. The nozzle should be kept screwed down firmly. The thong cleaner is identical with that for the service rifle, and should be used in the same manner.

RUPTURED CARTRIDGE EXTRACTOR, MARK II.

55. When a cartridge ruptures, it leaves the front end in the chamber, which telescopes over the bullet end of the next cartridge. As the operating handle is pulled back the live cartridge is extracted and ejected, sometimes withdrawing the ruptured fragment with it. In this case the use of the ruptured cartridge extractor is unnecessary.

If the ruptured end is not extracted by the following cartridge, cock the rifle and remove the magazine. Then insert the ruptured-cartridge extractor through the ejection opening, and push it forward into the chamber. Let the bolt forward without excessive shock so that the extractor engages the rim of the ruptured-cartridge extractor. Then draw the operating handle back, extracting and ejecting the ruptured-cartridge extractor and the ruptured fragment of the cartridge case. This fragment can sometimes be removed from the extractor by depressing the front catches of the sleeve, but it will usually be necessary to unscrew and remove the spindle and sleeve from the head of the ruptured cartridge extractor. Two, and sometimes more, ruptures can be extracted before it is necessary to remove the fragments from the extractor sleeve.

Every precaution should be taken to avoid the loss of this very important tool. In case it does become lost, it will sometimes be possible to remove a ruptured cartridge case by the use of a cartridge which has been oiled or moistened and coated lightly at the front end with sand or dirt. Although the rifleman should know of this method, its use should be prohibited except in cases of urgent necessity, as the residue of grit may result in the scoring of the polished surface of the chamber.

COMBINATION TOOL.

56. The small spanner at the head of the combination tool is used to turn the gas cylinder, or the flash hider. Barrels which are not excessively tight in the receiver can be removed and replaced by the use of the larger spanner, although shop facilities are necessary for the proper accomplishment of this work.

On tools of the latest design the catch end of this large spanner is drawn out to provide a thin screw driver end, used for the removal of the smaller screws on the rifle, such as the butt plate screws, the swivel screws, and the rear sight screws. The position of this screw driver allows the use of a large amount of leverage. Extreme care should, therefore, be exercised to avoid the breakage of the screw driver point. The regular screw driver end is heavily made and may be used for the removal of the butt stock bolt and the forearm screws.

GAS CYLINDER CLEANING TOOL.

57. This tool is provided for the cleaning of the gas-operating mechanism. These parts should habitually be kept clean and oiled. For thorough cleaning remove the gas-cylinder tube, gas cylinder, and slide. Care should be exercised to avoid scoring or damaging the cylinder walls or the rings of the gas piston.

Using the tool as a hand reamer, insert the smooth end of the body into the cylinder, turning it to the right as it is advanced toward the cylinder head. As soon as it reaches the head, press down and give the tool a few turns to cut the carbon from the inside surface of the head. Then withdraw and reverse the tool, using the recess cutter as a gauge to remove the carbon from the recess at the forward end of the interior of the gas cylinder. This part should be thoroughly cleaned, especially that portion near the edge of the operating surface of the cylinder wall.

Using the drift point, clean the ports in the barrel, gas cylinder tube, and gas cylinder. Scrape the carbon from the face of the piston with the front cutting edge of the cleaning-tool body, and remove the deposit from between the piston rings with the drift point. The parts should then be washed in kerosene if this is available.

LUMINOUS SIGHTS, MARK III.

58. The luminous sights are made of light spring steel, the sighting portions carrying glass tubes in which a radium luminous powder is sealed. These sights are delicate attachments and should be handled as such. Special attention should be given to keeping the luminous surface of the glass tubes clean. The steel portions should be kept lightly oiled to prevent rust. The luminous sights may be quickly attached to the permanent sights on the rifle. Their specific use is for night firing and the men should be trained in attaching and detaching them in the dark or when blindfolded.

To attach the sights snap the luminous front sight over the front-sight carrier, allowing the luminous front-sight body to automatically position itself over the front-sight blade. Care should be taken to insure that the circular sections of the luminous front sight spring properly around the front-sight carrier. Attach the rear luminous sight to the rear-sight slide by hooking the upper spring under the upper crosspiece of the rear-sight slide and pressing with thumb on the lower protecting shelf of the luminous rear sight, thereby compressing the spring and allowing the lower catch to engage over the peep sight of the rear-sight slide. The luminous rear sight is then in position and the peephole is registered with the peephole of the rear-sight slide.

To detach the luminous sights, lift the luminous front sight upward off the front-sight carrier. Remove the luminous rear sight by pressing upward on the lower shelf until the lower catch is released.

IMMEDIATE ACTION.

(Classroom instruction.)

INTRODUCTION.

59. The instructor will give definition of immediate action. (The automatic and instinctive application of a probable remedy for a stoppage, based on the position of the hammer pin, as determined by pulling back operating handle.)

DEMONSTRATION—EXPLANATION.

60. The instructor will demonstrate the four positions of the hammer pin and how to determine its position by pulling back the operating handle until it strikes the hammer pin.

61. Each member of team is required to learn how to determine the position of the hammer pin by setting the slide in the four positions (recoil spring removed and piston held) and then by placing thumb in rear of trigger guard and fingers on operating handle, squeezing operating handle back until it strikes the hammer pin. Students will then be required to state in which position mechanism was stopped.

62. (1) The instructor prepares the various stoppages for the first position of the hammer pin.

    (2) Explains the immediate action.

    (3) Requires each member of the squad to perform immediate action.

    (4) Examines members of the squad.

Each phase of the first position is taught until all are proficient before proceeding to the next phase.

IMMEDIATE ACTION TABLES.

EXPLANATORY NOTES.

63. The following tables will be utilized in teaching immediate action, both in the classroom and on the range. In classroom work, stoppages will be set up, not in the soldier's sight, and when he inspects the gun he will find such conditions as would be present if that stoppage occurred during actual firing. On the range these stoppages will be set up so as to occur during firing.

64. Column I describes the four positions of the operating handle in which it will strike the hammer pin when drawn back. Plates show rearward position of the operating handle for each position. These positions, which afford a ready indication of the correct immediate action to be performed, must be recognized clearly by all members of the squad before instruction proceeds.

65. Column II gives a detailed description of the immediate action to be performed as soon as the position of the hammer pin, by drawing back the operating handle, has been determined. This sequence of actions must be taught until instinctive. Pulling back the operating handle forms the first step in each case.

66. Column III names the stoppages which will occur in each given position, and Column IV gives the causes of these stoppages. Instructions should not proceed to this stage until it is certain that immediate action can be correctly and rapidly performed by each member of the squad.

67. A thorough knowledge of the causes of temporary stoppages will not only afford a practical knowledge of the operation of the rifle, but will also be an aid in the reduction of any unusual stoppage.

68. It is not essential to teach all soldiers the methods of setting up stoppages, but all instructors and assistants should understand this subject thoroughly.

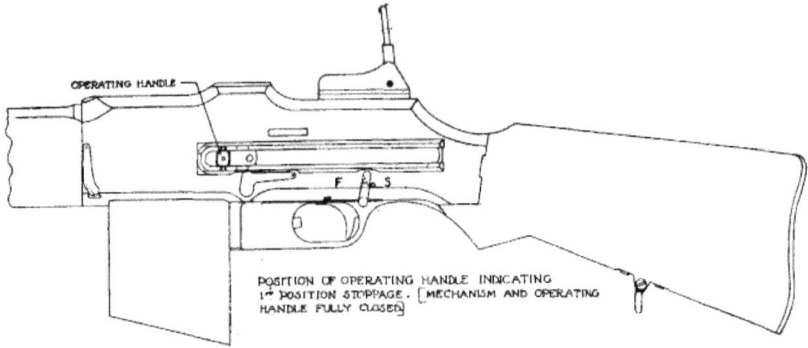

POSITION OF OPERATING HANDLE INDICATING
1st POSITION STOPPAGE. [MECHANISM AND OPERATING
HANDLE FULLY CLOSED]

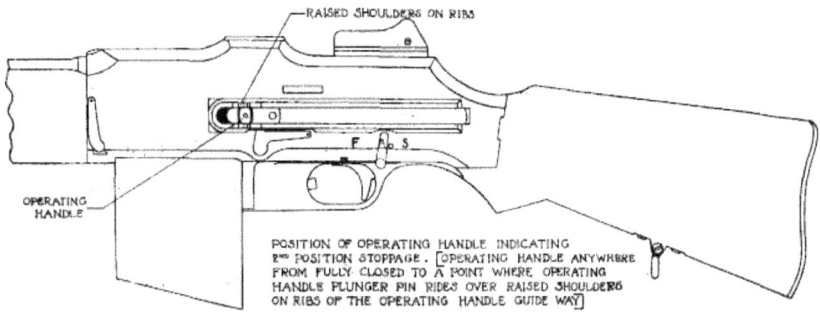

POSITION OF OPERATING HANDLE INDICATING
2nd POSITION STOPPAGE. [OPERATING HANDLE ANYWHERE
FROM FULLY CLOSED TO A POINT WHERE OPERATING
HANDLE PLUNGER PIN RIDES OVER RAISED SHOULDERS
ON RIBS OF THE OPERATING HANDLE GUIDE WAY]

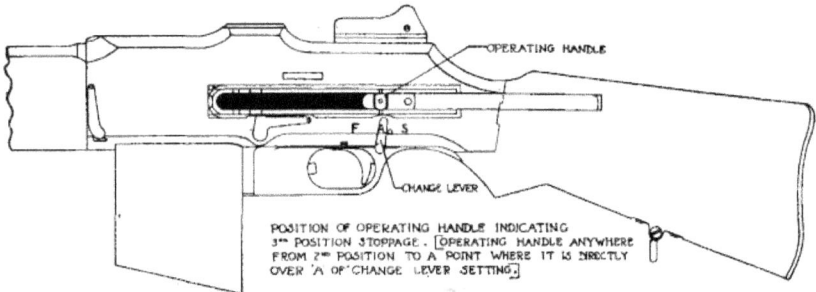

POSITION OF OPERATING HANDLE INDICATING
3rd POSITION STOPPAGE. [OPERATING HANDLE ANYWHERE
FROM 2nd POSITION TO A POINT WHERE IT IS DIRECTLY
OVER 'A' OF 'CHANGE' LEVER SETTING.]

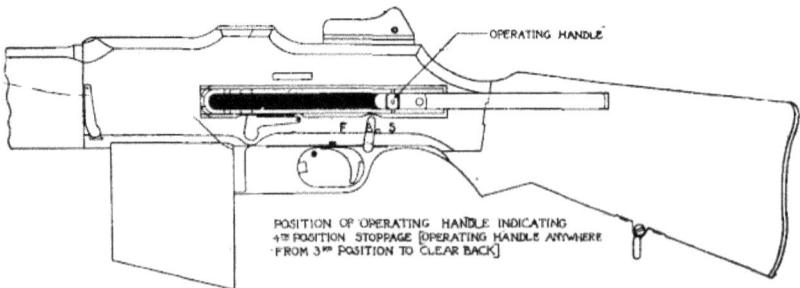

POSITION OF OPERATING HANDLE INDICATING
4th POSITION STOPPAGE [OPERATING HANDLE ANYWHERE
FROM 3rd POSITION TO CLEAR BACK]

Tables of immediate action for stoppages.

Position.	Immediate action.	Stoppage.	Causes.	Preparation for instruction.	
				Classroom (dummy ammunition).	Range (ball ammunition).
FIRST.					
Operating handle fully home.	I. Pull back operating handle, push magazine fully home, relay and fire. II. If stoppage recurs with rifle failing to fire, change firing pin and magazine.	A. Failure to fire. B. Failure to feed. A. Failure to fire. B. Failure to feed.	A. Defective ammunition. B. Magazine not fully home. 1. Broken firing pin. 2. Weak recoil spring. 3. Excessive friction. 1. Worn magazine catch. 2. Obstruction under lips of magazine. 3. Weak magazine spring. 4. Dirty or dented magazine.	A. Insert dummy round. B. Magazine not home. A. Insert broken firing pin. B. Obstruction under lips of magazine.	Same. Same. Same. Same.
	III. If stoppage recurs with rifle firing, regulate and clean gas ports.	A. Insufficient gas.	1. Gas ports not registered. 2. Gas ports clogged.	A. Failure to register gas ports.	Same.
SECOND.					
Operating handle strikes hammer pin between first position and the point at which operating handle plunger has ridden completely over raised shoulders on operating handle way.	I. Pull back operating handle, relay and fire. II. If stoppage recurs, pull back operating handle, feel face of bolt, receiver, and chamber, for extraneous matter and burrs, clean, relay and fire. III. If stoppage recurs, dismount rifle, examine bolt lock and bolt-lock recess for extraneous matter, clean, relay and fire.	A. Faulty ammunition. A. Obstruction or burred surface. A. Obstruction or burred surface.	A. Battered round. 1. Extraneous matter on face of bolt or in receiver. 2. Burrs in receiver or chamber. A. Extraneous matter or burrs on bolt lock or in bolt-lock recess.	A. Insert battered round. 1. Extraneous matter on face of bolt. 2. Do not set up. A. Do not set up.	Same. Same. Same. Same.
THIRD.					
Operating handle strikes hammer pin between second position and point directly over "A" on receiver.	I. Pull back operating handle, relay and fire. II. If stoppage recurs, pull back operating handle, remove magazine: A. If operating handle sticks, use defective cartridge extractor to remove ruptured case,[1] clean and oil chamber, oil cartridges, reload, relay and fire.	A. Faulty ammunition. A. Ruptured cartridge.	A. Battered round. A. Excessive headspace.	A. Insert round battered at shoulder. A. Insert front end of ruptured case in chamber.	Same. A. Use cartridge with groove filed ¼ inch from base.

[1] If no defective-cartridge extractor is available, oil the end of a cartridge and cover it with a small amount of dirt or sand, then place it in the chamber and let the bolt home on it. Ruptured cases may often be removed in this manner. Clean and oil chamber and bore very carefully after doing this.

Tables of immediate action for stoppages—Continued.

Position.	Immediate action.	Stoppage.	Causes.	Preparation for instruction.	
				Classroom (dummy ammunition).	Range (ball ammunition).
THIRD—continued. Operating handle strikes hammer pin between second position and point directly over "A" on receiver—Cont'd.	B. If operating handle comes back easily, remove case with cleaning rod, clean and oil chamber, feel for burr on shoulder of extractor, reload, relay and fire.	A. Failure to extract.	B. Dirty or dry chamber.	B. Insert cartridge with rim filed off.	Same.
	III. If stoppage recurs, pull back operating handle, remove magazine, feel face of bolt for protruding end of broken firing pin, remove cartridge, change firing pin, reload, relay and fire.	A. Failure to feed completely.	A. Broken firing pin.	A. Insert piece of metal to protrude beyond face of bolt.	A. Do not set up.
	IV. If mechanism sticks, remove trigger mechanism, and feel for obstruction between bolt supports and bolt. Remove same, assemble, reload, relay and fire.	A. Obstruction.	A. Extraneous matter between bolt and bolt supports.	A. Do not set up.	A. Same.
FOURTH. Operating handle strikes hammer pin between third position and as far back as it will go.	I. Pull back operating handle, remove magazine, feel for obstruction between ejector and bolt, remove same, reload, relay and fire.	A. Obstruction.	A. Extraneous matter between ejector and bolt.	A. Do not set up.	A. Same.
	II. If slide is not released by pulling trigger, remove trigger assembly, assemble properly, replace necessary parts, assemble, reload, relay and fire.	A. Improper assembly.	A. Middle prong of sear spring rides out of its channel, connector does not depress sear nose.	A. Assemble sear spring with middle prong out of channel.	A. Same.
		B. Broken part.	B. Middle prong of sear spring broken or bent.	B. Do not set up.	B. Same.

NOTES ON IMMEDIATE ACTION.

69. All stoppages which occur during firing may be classified under two main headings:

(1) *Temporary*, due to—

    A. Failure of some part of the rifle of which a duplicate is carried.

    B. Faulty ammunition.

    C. Neglect of observance of points listed for—before, during, and after firing. (Par. 86.)

    D. Ignorance on the part of the auto rifleman.

(2) *Prolonged*, which are due to failure of some part which can not be replaced or remedied in the field under fire, or without expert assistance or machine shop facilities.

Upon the training of the auto rifleman in immediate action depends the rapidity with which *temporary stoppages will be remedied*.

IMMEDIATE ACTION ON RANGE.

70. Stoppages will be set up on range, using prepared ammunition and parts so as to cause them to occur during firing. It is essential that stoppages be prepared accurately.

Student will fire. When stoppage occurs he will call *First position*, *Third position*, or whatever position he thinks it is. As soon as he has called the proper position, the instructor will command *Immediate action*, whereupon the soldier executes the necessary immediate action. If time permits it is well to have soldiers perform the function of instructor for other members of the squad.

71. When the soldier has been thoroughly grounded in immediate action by practice with individual stoppages he will be required to fire two or three prepared magazines which are loaded half with live rounds and half with rounds which will cause the various stoppages desired. He will perform immediate action in each case without command. He will keep on firing until the magazine is empty, and a record will be taken of the time necessary for this firing. In this manner all men will acquire speed and accuracy in reducing any stoppages which are likely to occur during actual firing. Table "A," immediate action table, will be fired at some time during work on the 1,000-inch range.

Table "A."

Position.	Fire.	Target.	Shots.	Range.
Prone	Semiautomatic	M. G. blank	1 prepared magazine	1,000-inch.
Prone	Automatic	M. G. blank	1 prepared magazine	1,000-inch.

NOTES ON STOPPAGES.

CAUSES.

72. Stoppages are caused by the following:

(1) Dirt (natural fouling incident to firing and also to careless cleaning).

(2) Insufficient oil (from failure to oil and because of oil burning up during firing).

(3) Extraneous matter in working parts. (Due to poor cleaning, brass chipped off from cartridges, breakages, blown primer, etc.)

(4) Improper assembly of rifle. (Gas ports not registered, middle prong of sear spring riding on one wall of sear carrier, etc.)

(5) Breakages. (Due to wrong assembly, oversize or undersize parts, burrs, incorrect heat treatment, overheating of parts incident to firing, etc.)

(6) Burred parts. Due to use of force, grit, etc., improper assembly, extraneous matter in mechanism.)

(7) Magazine troubles. (Due to bent or dented magazines, worn magazines, catch notch, extraneous matter, as blown primer, between lips of magazine and top cartridge.)

(8) Faulty ammunition. (Dented cartridges, failure of primer or charge, etc.)

(9) Excessive play in parts. (Due to wear in stripping parts not supposed to be stripped—as removing barrel from receiver, for instance.)

(10) Ruptured cartridges. (Due to excessive head space.) Head space is the distance between the face of the bolt and the shoulder of a standard steel test cartridge. If excessive head space exists when the cartridge is chambered properly, the cartridge case will be forced against the walls of the chamber at the instant of explosion. The cartridge case base will be driven to the rear, as it is not supported by the bolt. This results in rupture about one-half inch from the base of the cartridge. In effect the action during the period of gas pressure within the cartridge case is the same as if the chamber gripped all the outer surface of the cartridge case except the part about one-half inch near the head. The pressure within the cartridge case being 50,000 pounds per square inch, the ungripped portion of the case is torn from the gripped part and forced back against the face of the bolt. (The case is never pulled apart by extractor.)

Analysis of various stoppages (as to cause).

FIRST POSITION.

73. *Failure to feed.*—Obstruction (usually a blown primer) between lips of magazine and top cartridge causes failure of presentation of a cartridge to feed rib and the bolt goes home on an empty chamber. Same result occurs when the magazine catch notch becomes so worn as to permit the magazine to drop down slightly and also when magazine catch breaks, or when magazine is not pushed clear up in magazine opening.

74. *Failure to fire.*—Faulty primer or charge will cause a misfire, as will also a broken or short firing pin. Frequently the beginner will mistake a misfire due to an obstruction between the face of the bolt and the breech for one due to a broken firing pin. He should remember that the latter is a first-position stoppage and the former a second-position stoppage. A misfire due to a broken firing pin will not show any indentation on the primer. The second-position stoppage almost invariably shows a slight indentation.

75. *Insufficient gas.*—A stoppage in the first position with an empty case in the chamber is due to insufficient gas, which in turn may be due to the gas ports not being properly registered or being partially clogged, or to excessive friction because of lack of oil and dirty chamber.

SECOND POSITION.

76. *Failure to fire.*—A deformed round bulged near the base or an obstruction lodging between face of bolt and the breech, thus holding firing pin away from primer. Primer will be slightly dented. This stoppage is typical. When the piece stops in the second position always look for an obstruction either on the face of the bolt or in breech recess where bolt and receiver join. Most frequent obstruction is the blown primer. Often it is difficult to see. Frequently it drops off as the bolt is drawn back. If the stoppage recurs it is sure that an obstruction is in the rifle between the face of the bolt and the breech or between bolt lock and receiver top plate.

THIRD POSITION.

77. *Ruptured case.*—This stoppage is due to excessive head space. When the immense pressure following the ignition of the charge is taken up by the cartridge case, if this case is not properly supported by the bolt it will rupture about five-eighths of an inch from the base.

The short end at the base will then be extracted and the larger portion of the case will remain in the barrel. A temporary correction for such a stoppage is to clean and oil the chamber thoroughly and oil the cartridges.

78. *Broken firing pin.*—This stoppage is caused by the end of a broken firing pin protruding through the firing pin hole in the face of the bolt. The cartridge is then kept from sliding under the extractor as the bolt moves forward and a third-position stoppage will result. The cartridge will show an abrasion near the base. To remedy this stoppage the firing pin must be replaced.

Mechanism wedged fast in third position.—This is a rare stoppage. Slide can not be moved forward or backward. It occurs when any obstruction gets between one of the bolt supports and the bolt lock. As the slide is driven to the rear the bolt lock is wedged fast by the obstruction. This stoppage has been caused by blown primer or by a piece of metal broken off the rear of the firing pin channel wall. It should be reduced in a properly equipped shop.

FOURTH POSITION.

79. One fourth-position stoppage is when a blown primer wedges itself between the points of the ejector and the face of the bolt, thereby holding the bolt and mechanism back in the fourth position.

80. The other fourth-position stoppage is that in which the piece is cocked and the trigger mechanism will not release the sear when set at " A " or " F." This is due to a broken sear spring, a broken or lost connector, and improper assembling of the sear spring, or to any cause which has the effect of moving the middle prong of the sear spring too far to the front with respect to the connector, so that the connector is not cammed under the tail of the sear.

CARE AND ADJUSTMENT.

REGULATIONS CONCERNING HANDLING THE RIFLE.

81. All men must have impressed upon their minds the vital necessity for properly caring for this weapon. They must understand and appreciate that, in order to render efficient service, a most careful cleaning and oiling is necessary at all times, especially in the field. The rifle should be kept in the carrying case when not in use, in order to minimize the accumulation of dirt, mud, and rust in the mechanism, which may cause the rifle to fail to function.

CLEANING.

THE BARREL.

The life of the barrel should be about 8,000 rounds if it is not fired more than 200 rounds at a time.

The barrel should never be removed until completely worn out.

The barrel should be cleaned with sal soda solution (20 per cent hot solution) to remove powder fouling, and with ammonia preparation to remove metallic fouling.

NOTE.—*The ammonia preparation is to be used only under the supervision of an officer, or an experienced noncommissioned officer designated by organization commander.*

Ammonia preparation.—One-half teaspoon ammonium persulphate, one-half teaspoon ammonium carbonate, one-half pint 30 per cent ammonia, one-fourth pint water, one-eighth teaspoon potassium bichromate.

Procedure.—Place cork in chamber and plug up gas port. Pour in solution until barrel is full, after adding a few drops of sperm oil, which prevents ammonia from evaporating. Do not permit solution to remain in barrel longer than two hours. While the solution is acting, small bubbles come to the surface and the solution turns blue. When bubbles stop rising, remove solution. After the use of this solution, the bore should be thoroughly cleaned and saturated with 20 per cent sal soda solution, then dried and coated with a thin film of oil.

OTHER PARTS.

All parts must be clean and free from grit in order to avoid excessive wear.

All powder fouling must be removed from gun to insure proper functioning.

Rifle should be dismounted, and all parts wiped dry and clean, after which they should be covered with a thin coating of oil.

The gas cylinder, piston, and all parts coming in contact with gas should be cleaned with sal soda solution, wiped dry, and coated with a light film of oil.

Magazines should be carefully watched to avoid denting or bending during transportation or handling.

Rifles to be shipped or stored for any considerable time should be cleaned, oiled, and cosmolined.

82. The following regulations are prescribed regarding the handling of the Browning automatic rifle:

(1) Force will not be used in stripping and assembling.

(2) This piece will not be stripped nor assembled against time.

(3) The bore and working parts will be kept thoroughly cleaned and oiled.

(4) The magazine will receive the same care as the rifle. Every effort will be made to prevent bending or denting the magazines, being especially careful of the lips and magazine catch notch.

(5) The filing or altering of shape or parts will not be permitted.

83. The rifle is so constructed as to be taken apart and put together easily. Most parts are designed with a view to prevent wrong assembling. Where difficulty arises in stripping and assembling easily it is due to error on the part of the soldier, and the use of force will only result in damage to the rifle.

The practice of stripping and assembling against time serves no useful purpose and results in burring and damaging parts. Gradual skill develops as men become more familiar with the rifle, and lost motion is eliminated. Men should be taught in stripping to lay out parts in obvious sequence of assembling, and should so thoroughly learn the rifle that taking it apart and putting it together are matters of second nature.

Lubrication is necessary to the operation of the rifle. Dirt and extraneous matter will prevent it from functioning and do it damage. Instruction in care and preservation should be so thorough that cleaning and oiling become a matter of habit.

Unless strict supervision is exercised, inexperienced men, and sometimes experienced men, will file or otherwise alter parts which do not need it. This results in damage to the rifle and usually fails to remedy trouble. Filing and altering of parts are sometimes necessary, but should never be done except by an expert, under direction of an officer competent to supervise the work.

Use for instruction in mechanism is hard on rifles. This fact should be borne in mind and, in the company, after the completion of the first course in mechanism, only a limited number of rifles should be so used.

POINTS TO BE OBSERVED.

84. Before firing:
  (1) Test trigger mechanism at safe, (A), and (F).
  (2) See that bore is clear and clean.
  (3) Work slide back and forth rapidly several times to see that it moves freely and does not stick.
  (4) Test ejector and extractor with dummy or empty case.
  (5) Verify proper setting of gas port.
  (6) Verify oiling.
  (7) Verify cleaning.
  (8) Examine magazines and eliminate faulty ones.
  (9) See that kit contains oil can full of oil and full complement of spare parts.

85. During firing:
  (1) Keep magazines and chamber protected from dirt.
  (2) Do not allow rifle to become dry.
  (3) Clean bore and gas system frequently.

86. After firing:
  (1) Remove loaded magazine.
  (2) Let bolt forward.
  (3) Wipe out bore and oil rifle.
  (4) Thoroughly clean rifle at first opportunity.
  (5) Replenish spare parts.
  (6) Reload magazines as soon as possible.

GAS ADJUSTMENT.

87. The rifle should normally be operated on the smallest port, and this setting will never be varied unless the rifle shows signs of insufficient gas. To align the smallest port, screw in the gas cylinder with the combination tool until the shoulder of the gas cylinder is about one turn from the corresponding shoulder of the gas cylinder tube, and the smallest circle on the cylinder head is toward the barrel. Lock the cylinder in position. If, upon firing, the rifle shows signs of insufficient gas, try setting the cylinder one complete turn on each side of the original setting. As soon as the proper setting has been obtained the rifleman will carefully note the position so that he can quickly assemble the cylinder to the proper point without trial.

The larger ports are provided for use in case of emergency, when the action of the rifle has been made sluggish through the collection of dirt and grit, or the lack of oil, and the conditions render it impossible for the riflemen to correct these troubles. For this reason the threads should be kept clean and oiled and the cylinder free to turn if necessary. The extractor, ejector, and the chamber of the barrel should be examined and cleaned and defects corrected when possible. Under adverse conditions, and when signs of insufficient gas become apparent, the cylinder should be unscrewed one-third of a turn, thus registering the medium circle and aligning the medium port with the gas orifice. Repeat this operation in order to connect the largest port with the barrel.

Excessive friction or dirt may sometimes result in the failure of the action to complete the forward movement under the action of the recoil spring, which part may also have become permanently set or short from continued use under conditions of excessive heat. In such case replace the recoil spring.

RESULTS OF INSUFFICIENT GAS.

(1) Failure to recoil (usually due to a misaligned or excessively clogged gas port, or extremely dirty mechanism).

(2) Failure to eject.

(3) Weak ejection.

(4) Uncontrolled automatic fire (exceptional).

RESULTS OF TOO MUCH GAS.

(1) Excessive speed, causing pounding.

(2) Excessive heat in gas operating mechanism.

NOTES FOR REPAIRMEN.

88. The following notes are prepared for the use of repairmen: Filing, or otherwise altering parts, should only be done under the strictest supervision, as this often fails to remedy the trouble and results in damage to the rifle. Filing and altering of parts are sometimes necessary, but should never be done except by an expert repairman, under the direction of a commissioned officer competent to supervise the work. All defective parts should be distinctly marked or tagged to avoid their future use.

BARREL.

89. The barrel should not be removed until worn to such an extent as to require replacement. This wear usually occurs in the rifling near the breech or in the chamber. A barrel is usually good for 8,000 rounds, after which time the accuracy depreciates quite rapidly. A worn or pitted chamber may result in ruptured shells, or in the shells swelling and sticking in the chamber, rendering extraction difficult or uncertain.

The gas port through the barrel and gas cylinder tube bracket may become stopped up and not allow sufficient gas to pass through to insure positive action. To remedy this difficulty clear the port with the gas cylinder cleaning tool. The lower surface, especially that portion immediately surrounding the port of the gas cylinder tube bracket, should fit closely to the corresponding surface of the gas cylinder tube. Some wear at this point can be taken up by bending the lips of the bracket down slightly, tapping them lightly with a hammer, or by bending the retaining rib of the tube back at each edge, thus bringing the surfaces into closer contact. A smooth, close fit is desired. If the fit is excessively tight, some metal may be removed from the surface of the gas cylinder tube bracket by the use of the special hand scraper provided for this purpose, or with an oilstone or dead smooth file. Care should be exercised not to remove too much metal, especially from that surface near the port.

GAS OPERATING MECHANISM.

90. The front retaining rib of the gas cylinder tube may become too loose in the gas cylinder tube bracket, resulting in insufficient gas and requiring adjustment as described above, or replacement. The wall of the tube may become dented, thus binding the piston. In some cases it may be possible to straighten this out until the piston works freely. In replacing a gas cylinder tube see that it correctly fits the bracket and that the rear hole lines up properly in the receiver. The tube should never be twisted to secure a fit at this point. In case of necessity a reamer may be run through the rear hole to clean out a small amount of metal.

The ports of the gas cylinder may become clogged to such an extent as to render the action uncertain, or burnt powder deposited on the inside of the gas cylinder, causing the piston to stick. The gas cylinder cleaning tool may be used to clean these parts. Failure to operate, due to insufficient gas, is sometimes the result of wrong assembling of the gas cylinder, screwing it in one turn from the shoulder. Unscrew one-third of a turn to change to the medium port, and one-third of a turn farther to the large port. The relative sizes of the ports are indicated by circles on the front end of the cylinder. The threads of the gas cylinder should fit snugly enough to prevent excessive gas leakage. The fit of the gas cylinder and piston, although free, should not be excessively loose, in order that the recoil may be uniform. Extreme wear would necessitate replacement. In replacing a gas cylinder make sure that the piston works freely when the cylinder is set at each port. Test as described below.

If the gas piston has become bent it may bind in the gas cylinder or tube. Slight bends may be straightened and tested in the following manner: Remove the trigger guard, bolt, and recoil spring. The piston and slide should work back and forth easily as the muzzle of the rifle is tilted first up and then down. Particular attention should be given at the point where the piston enters the cylinder. In replacing a piston, the new one should be tested in this manner. In the case of the old type piston, which is threaded rigidly into the slide, slight bending may be necessary in order to secure the proper alignment.

RECEIVER.

91. Wear in the receiver usually occurs on the locking surface or on the bolt supports. The rear cam surface of the bolt supports must be accurately positioned in order to cam the bolt lock upward at the proper time. The bolt supports must fit tightly in the receiver and be well riveted. The hammer used in riveting should be heavy enough to swell the rivets throughout their entire length. An excessively loaded cartridge may spread the side of the receiver slightly and loosen the bolt supports. In this case the sides of the receiver should be carefully brought back into position, with the aid of a vise, and the bolt supports reriveted.

FIRING MECHANISM.

92. The slide should fit freely in the receiver and the sides should be straight. The slide should not be excessively loose in the receiver, as this may cause the hammer pin to batter the top of the front end of the slot in the left side of the receiver, rendering it difficult to pull back the operating handle when cocking the rifle. To remedy this difficulty the slot can be smoothed over and widened slightly by filing. Slight cracks may occur in the slide, extending from the hammer pin hole to the upper surface. This does not in general affect the operation of the rifle.

The hammer should have a good bearing against the seat in the rear of the slide, and when assembled should not be loose enough to allow any appreciable tilting when pressure is exerted in the upper portion of the front face. In addition to this condition, excessive wear or deformation of the front face may be the cause of misfires. When the parts are in their forward position the hammer should clear the firing pin, but not by more than one thirty-second of an inch. The hammer should come up against the link when the gas cylinder tube is not in place. The recoil spring should not become set, and hence too short for positive operation. In some cases this can be corrected temporarily by pulling out the spring. In some cases replacements will be necessary. The recoil spring should be 15 inches long.

In addition to the actual length of the firing pin the following points determine the distance which the firing pin will protrude through the bolt in the locked position (causing pierced primers at one extreme and misfires at the other) : The distance from the face of the hammer to its rear bearing surface against the slide, the distance from this surface to the front stop shoulder of the slide, the distance from the slide stop shoulder of the gas cylinder tube to the gas cylinder tube retaining pin hole, the distance from this hole to the face of the receiver, the distance from the face of the receiver to the locking surface and the distance from the locking surface of the bolt lock to the front face of the bolt. Firing pin protrusion can only be gauged when the rifle is assembled and the bolt is in the locked position. It will be necessary to use a gauge extending from the muzzle of the gun, or to take a wax impression of the projection when the bolt is locked.

When the bolt is unlocked the link should bear on the locking shoulder of the bolt lock, and should hold the bolt lock up so that it just clears the bolt supports and guide as the bolt is moved rearward. Frequent blown or pierced primers may cause the rear head of the firing pin to batter the front of the link. This battered surface should not be allowed to develop a sharp edge which might catch or break off the head of the firing pin.

The top rear corner of the firing pin head should be well rounded to avoid the above-mentioned breakage. The shank of the firing pin should be straight and the point not excessively deformed or pitted. The retracting cam should be beveled on each side, and neither this part nor the corresponding slot in the bolt lock should show battering or signs of misalignment.

The bolt and bolt lock are an assembled unit and should never be separated. There should be a good bearing between the two so that none of the shock of the recoil is taken on the bolt lock pin. The bolt lock pin may become loose with wear until one end projects and catches on the inside of the receiver, resulting in stoppages and mutilation of the receiver. Test by pushing the pin both ways with the finger. It should not be possible to cause it to project on either side. In case of projection, rerivet the pin. Considerable wear on the locking shoulder of the bolt lock, in the joint between the bolt and bolt lock, or on the face of the bolt, may result in excessive head-space, causing ruptured cartridges and, in some cases, blown primers. During the rearward motion the bolt lock should never bear to any appreciable extent on the bolt supports or guide. If the firing pin hole in the face of the bolt is enlarged or off center, the assembly should be replaced, as this is often the cause of breakage of firing pin points.

When the gun is assembled without the recoil spring, but with the gas cylinder and gas cylinder tube in place, the recoiling parts should slide back and forth freely as the gun is turned muzzle up and vice versa, unless the breeching is snug. In that case they should move freely when the bolt lock is disengaged from the recoil shoulder of the receiver. On the forward movement the bolt lock should be cammed up by the rounded rear ends of the bolt supports, but there should be sufficient clearance between the bolt supports and the locking shoulder of the receiver to prevent excessive binding. When in the locked position the front shoulder of the bolt should just clear the rear shoulder of the barrel. If the bolt comes up against the barrel, but does not interfere with the locking of the bolt lock, the operation of the gun will not be affected unless dirt is allowed to accumulate in front of the bolt.

The extractor should have particular attention to see that it has retained its proper shape and that the cartridge fits the hook correctly. The inner radius of the extractor hook should closely fit the bottom of the cannelure of the cartridge. The extractor notch just back of the hook should be deep enough to allow the extractor to come down into the cannelure, so that minimum cartridge will snap in and be held up firmly in place. Faulty ejection may result if the cartridge is allowed to drop even a short distance. To test this, remove the bolt and firing pin and insert a live cartridge under the extractor. It should be able to withstand considerable shaking without dropping down out of place. Examine to see if the extractor hook bears against the bottom of the cannelure at all points and that the base of the cartridge is held snugly against the face of the bolt. About 0.01 of an inch clearance between the base of the cartridge and the bolt face will not in general affect the operation of the rifle, but more than this may cause weak ejection. The lower corners of the extractor and lips of the bolt should be slightly rounded so as not to chip brass from the cartridges as they slip up into place. The rear face of the notch in the extractor, which bears against the lug of the bolt during extraction, should be slightly undercut, thus tending to prevent the extractor from slipping over the rim of the cartridge or from pulling out. The rear face of the extractor hook should be square and the extracting edges fairly sharp. An excessive amount of dirt under the extractor may result in failure to extract or failure to eject. The extractor should be a snug fit in the bolt. Side play or twisting is especially liable to cause trouble. Worn or defective

REAR SIGHT BASE

BOLT LOCK

BOLT

FIRING PIN

LINK

RECEIVER

CARTRIDGE

BARREL

HAMMER

SLIDE

SEAR SPRING

SEAR

POSITION OF BOLT, BOLT LOCK
AND TRIGGER MECHANISM AT
INSTANT OF FIRING.

SEAR CARRIER

TRIGGER

CONNECTOR

MAGAZINE CATCH

MAGAZINE RELEASE

TRIGGER GUARD

LOCKING RECESS

BOLT LOCK

BOLT

FIRING PIN

LINK

HAMMER

SLIDE

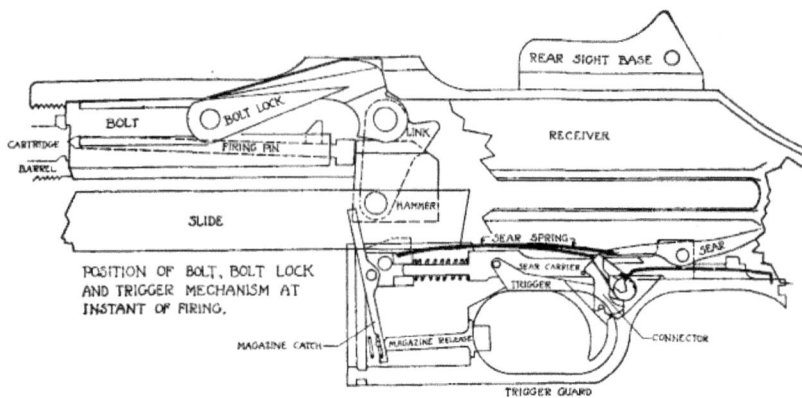

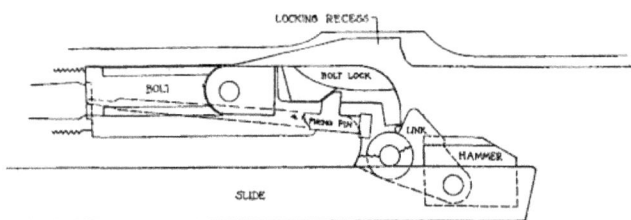

SHOWING UNLOCKING OF BOLT AND WITHDRAWAL OF FIRING PIN

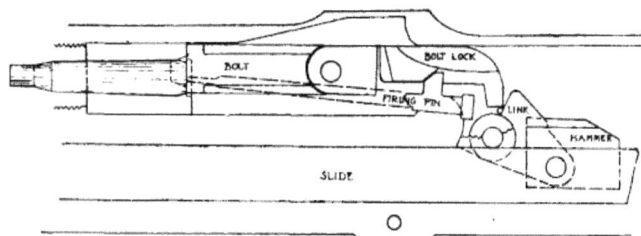

BOLT LOCK

BOLT

FIRING PIN

LINK

HAMMER

SLIDE

SHOWING FURTHER MOTION OF RECOILING PORTIONS TO REAR AND EXTRACTION
OF CARTRIDGE CASE

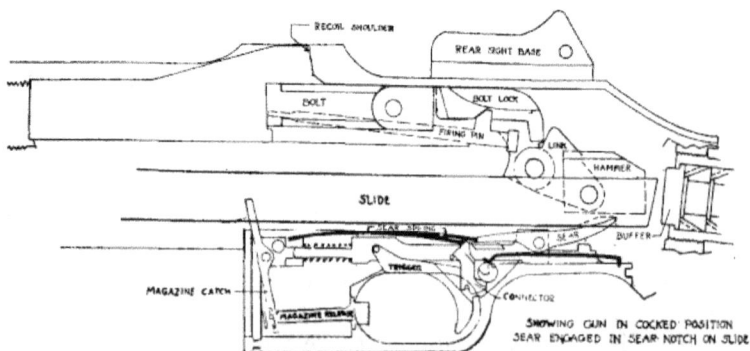

RECOIL SHOULDER

REAR SIGHT BASE

BOLT

BOLT LOCK

FIRING PIN

LINK

HAMMER

SLIDE

SEAR SPRING

SEAR

BUFFER

MAGAZINE CATCH

TRIGGER

CONNECTOR

MAGAZINE RELEASE

SHOWING GUN IN COCKED POSITION
SEAR ENGAGED IN SEAR NOTCH ON SLIDE

extractors may often be corrected by proper and careful filing. The extractor spring rarely causes any trouble.

TRIGGER GUARD MECHANISM.

93. The fit of the trigger guard in the receiver is not important except that it should be fairly snug sideways. The sear should be a loose fit in the sear carrier. The nose of the sear, as well as the sear notch in the slide, should be correct in shape in order to maintain positive engagement. The sear pin should carry the tension of the counter-recoil spring, leaving the trigger pin free. The trigger should be a loose fit in the trigger guard and the connector loose in the trigger. The trigger pull should be smooth and from 6 to 10 pounds. The change lever should work smoothly. The ideal condition in semiautomatic fire is for the cam on the connector to engage the sear carrier just at the moment the sear releases the slide. The sear spring should fit in the trigger guard without an excessive amount of slide play. The center leaf should have a smooth and continuous bearing against the bevel surface of the connector. The magazine catch should work freely and easily and should hold the magazine up closely to the bolt supports.

The ejector should fit fairly close in the trigger-guard guides. An excessive amount of play forward and backward may result in weak ejection. This can sometimes be corrected by bending the ejector slightly. The upper end of the ejector should spring slightly when pressed back. The location of the working end of the ejector for height and side position is of primary importance. To examine this, draw back the mechanism until the bolt face is even with the ejector. The ejector should fit up within one thirty-second of an inch of the bolt but should not bind. A poor fitting ejector can be corrected by bending until it fits up closely in the notch of the bolt. The upper part of the ejector should not bend rearward. If the ejection is correct the shells will be given a spinning motion as they leave the rifle and will be thrown diagonally forward with considerable force. Test the ejection with a magazine filled with dummies. First operate the rifle slowly by hand, which should result in positive ejection. Then operate rapidly, when the cartridge should be ejected with force.

REAR SIGHT.

94. If the rear sight is properly assembled with a good driving fit it will give little trouble. If the sight works loose from the receiver it may be necessary to replace the sight base. It may, however, be possible to swell the dovetail of the rear sight base by light and careful peening with a hammer until the necessary drive fit is obtained.

BUFFER ASSEMBLY.

95. If properly assembled the buffer tube assembly will cause little or no difficulty. Special attention should be given to see that the buffer spring is always assembled behind the buffer friction cups and cones. The bronze buffer friction cups sometimes split and in this case should be replaced.

MAGAZINES.

96. Magazines should fit easily in the receiver and should be free enough to drop out under their own weight. The form of the inturned lips is important. Cartridges should strip out smoothly and without excessive friction, which might hold back the bolt to such an extent as to cause failure to breech and misfires. The inside distance between the pressed-in ribs should be maintained within reasonable limits. The magazine follower should work freely. Deformed or battered magazines may be repaired by placing over the salvaging tools and bringing back into shape with a lead hammer.

97. Probable causes of failure to extract:
(1) Defective extractor.
(2) Dirt under extractor.
(3) Dirt in chamber.
(4) Pitted chamber.
(5) Weak extractor spring.
(6) Defective ammunition.

98. Probable causes of failure to eject:
(1) Insufficient gas.
(2) Defective extractor.
(3) Dirt under extractor.
(4) Ejector does not fit up close to bolt.
(5) Ejector binds on bolt.
(6) Ejector has too much backward play.
(7) Ejector bent backward or otherwise defective.
(8) Weak extractor spring.
(9) Defective ammunition.

99. Probable causes of failure to breech:
(1) Dirt between bolt and rear end of barrel.
(2) Primer in mechanism, generally in front of bolt.
(3) Defective bolt lock or pin.
(4) Defective magazine.
(5) Piston binding.
(6) Excessive friction.
(7) Recoil spring too short.

100. Probable causes of insufficient gas:

    (1) Ports clogged.

    (2) Poor fit between gas cylinder tube and bracket.

    (3) Gas leakage around piston (worn cylinder).

    (4) Piston binding, or cylinder dirty.

    (5) Gas cylinder threaded in too far, or vice versa.

    (6) Excessive friction.

101. Probable causes of ruptured cartridges:

    (1) Locking surface of bolt lock worn.

    (2) Bearing between bolt and bolt lock worn.

    (3) Face of bolt worn.

    (4) Chamber of barrel worn or pitted.

    (5) Locking shoulder of receiver worn.

    (6) Bolt supports loose or worn.

    (7) Defective ammunition.

BROWNING AUTOMATIC RIFLE INSPECTIONS.

102. Careful and frequent inspections of the automatic rifle and its accessories should be made. Shortages of spare parts must be filled. Platoon commanders will be held responsible for the automatic rifles of their platoons being in excellent condition at all times.

The following detailed instruction will be an aid to all platoon commanders. Rifle stripped and cleaned, inspect each part for following points:

RECEIVER AND BARREL.

(1) Tightness of flash hider and front sight.
(2) Condition of bore.
(3) Tightness and alignment of barrel.
(4) Burrs on receiver or any part.
(5) Position of bolt guide and spring.
(6) Tightness of buffer tube.
(7) Tightness of stock.

REAR SIGHT.

(1) Firmness of rear sight base.
(2) Free movement of slide.
(3) Condition of slide catch spring.

GAS CYLINDER AND TUBE.

(1) Proper alignment of gas ports.
(2) Fouling of gas cylinder.
(3) Burrs.

GAS PISTON AND SLIDE.

(1) Fouling of piston.
(2) Sear notch for chips and burrs.
(3) Hammer pin for looseness. (Should be loose.)
(4) Length of recoil spring. (15 inches.)

BOLT GROUP.

(1) Proper fitting of extractor.
(2) Security of bolt-lock pin.
(3) Clearance for firing pin in face of bolt.
(4) Bolt and bolt lock for wear and burrs.
(5) Shoulder of firing pin to see that it is cammed easily and in alignment, by cutout portion on under side of bolt lock.

TRIGGER GUARD GROUP.

(1) Length and strength of sear spring.
(2) Wear and burrs on all parts.
(3) Verify presence of all springs.
(4) Worn magazine catch.

MAGAZINE.

(1) Shape of magazine lips.
(2) Dirty or dented parts.
(3) Fitting of magazine in receiver.
(4) Wear in magazine-catch notch.

103. After rifle is assembled, test for proper assembly and action, especially trigger mechanism, and piston in gas cylinder.

BLANK AMMUNITION ATTACHMENTS FOR BROWNING AUTOMATIC RIFLE.

(See cut, page 89.)

104. Blank ammunition attachments for functioning the automatic rifle have been developed in order to use the automatic rifle in maneuvers and for such purposes as the gun will be used to simulate service firing. The blank ammunition attachments are adapted to fire model of 1909, blank ammunition. The blank ammunition, model of 1909, is slightly modified by crimping the end of the shell case slightly to facilitate the feeding in the magazine. The same ammunition is used with the Browning machine gun, model of 1917. This type of ammunition supersedes the old type, model of 1909 ammunition, and is being manufactured exclusively, inasmuch as it will function in service rifles, machine guns, and automatic rifles. The blank ammunition attachments for the Browning automatic rifle consist of:

1. Muzzle piece.
2. Gas cylinder tube retaining pin and safety (assembled).
    (*a*) Gas cylinder tube retaining pin.
    (*b*) Gas cylinder tube retaining pin key.
    (*c*) Gas cylinder tube retaining pin safety.
3. Magazine (blank ammunition).
    (*a*) Magazine tube (standard altered).
    (*b*) Magazine follower (standard altered).
    (*c*) Cartridge guide (new).
    (*d*) Magazine spring (same as standard).
    (*e*) Magazine base (same as standard).

105. *Muzzle piece.*—The muzzle piece is a cylindrical bar about 2 inches long with a raised annular ring around the center shaped like a top; one end is tapped and threaded to fit the Browning automatic rifle barrel. The inside of the tapped end is conical shape, through which is drilled a small hole. A wrench slot is also provided similar to the flash hider for assembling and disassembling. The muzzle piece resembles the flash hider in that the flash hider is removed and the muzzle piece is screwed on the barrel in its place. The peculiar toplike shape is made in order to readily distinguish the muzzle piece, so that it will not be left on the gun by mistake. The conical shape allows the gases from the explosion to be trapped and to burn the wad from the cartridge case.

106. *Gas cylinder tube retaining pin and safety assembly.*—The gas cylinder tube retaining pin and safety assembly is very similar in operation to the gas cylinder tube retaining pin used with the automatic rifle. An additional arm is provided as a safety. When the gas cylinder tube retaining pin and safety is assembled to the gun the safety arm extends into the magazine space of the rifle. The pointed nose of the safety is then in such a position that the blank ammunition magazine only can be fed into the gun.

107. *Magazine (blank ammunition).*—The magazine for firing blank ammunition operates principally the same as the standard magazine. The loading tool provided with the Browning magazine will serve to load the blank ammunition from clips into the blank ammunition magazine. The blank ammunition magazine is made up by altering the standard Browning magazine and inserting the cartridge guide to guide the blank cartridge from the magazine and to block out service ammunition from the magazine. A V slot is made in the left side of the magazine to allow clearance for the safety on the gas cylinder tube retaining pin. This gives additional safety by blocking out the service magazine, which would otherwise make it possible to load service ammunition into the gun. The standard service magazine follower is used with the changes noted. The magazine spring and base are the same as are used in the service magazine. The insertion of the magazine requires the least bit of training as the lower part of the magazine must be tipped slightly to the left side of the gun to allow the safety to enter the slot of the magazine. This is made necessary in order to reenforce the magazine at the top of the V slot. This could be eliminated by extending the slot to the edge of the magazine; however, this would have left it too weak. Should the magazine feed the cartridge too high to enter the chamber properly, a slight closing in of the lips of the magazine or a forcing down of the cartridge guide slightly, will eliminate this malfunction.

108. The following instructions will be strictly adhered to:

Before inserting the blank ammunition in the automatic rifle, first observe the cartridge to make sure that it is a blank cartridge. The space for the top cartridge will allow one service round of ammunition to be fed into the magazine. Two service cartridges can be fed into the blank ammunition magazine. However, when the bolt goes forward, the two service cartridges bind against the cartridge guide, which prevents their feeding. When, by accident, a single round, top cartridge, is fed into the magazine, *it will feed*, and every precaution must be taken to make sure the top cartridge in the magazine is a blank.

109. All magazines loaded with blanks must be inspected before inserting in the gun. The safety on the gas cylinder tube retaining pin will block out the service magazine, thereby making it safe against loading service ammunition in the gun.

110. With the Browning automatic rifle made ready for firing, remove the gas cylinder tube retaining pin, insert the gas cylinder tube retaining pin and safety assembly. Make sure the gun is not loaded, remove the flash hider, and screw the muzzle piece in position with the combination tool. Load the magazine in the ordinary manner except use blank ammunition, model of 1909. This will be packed in paper cartons marked " 20 cal. .30 blank cartridges, model of 1909, for service rifles, models of 1903 and 1917, automatic rifle with muzzle attachment and machine gun with muzzle attachment." The note " Dangerous within 20 feet " applies to rifles and machine guns when fired without these attachments. When fired with the attachments, they are perfectly safe within 5 to 10 feet. To remove the blank ammunition attachments, remove the muzzle piece first and the gas cylinder tube retaining pin and safety assembly last. The blank ammunition attachments and the rifle after firing should be thoroughly cleaned with pure water, then soda solution if available, then dried thoroughly and oiled. Ammonia solution need not be used after firing blank ammunition, as there is no metal fouling to be removed. In case water or soda solution is not immediately available after firing, a thorough oiling of the parts will prevent corrosion until cleaning facilities are at hand.

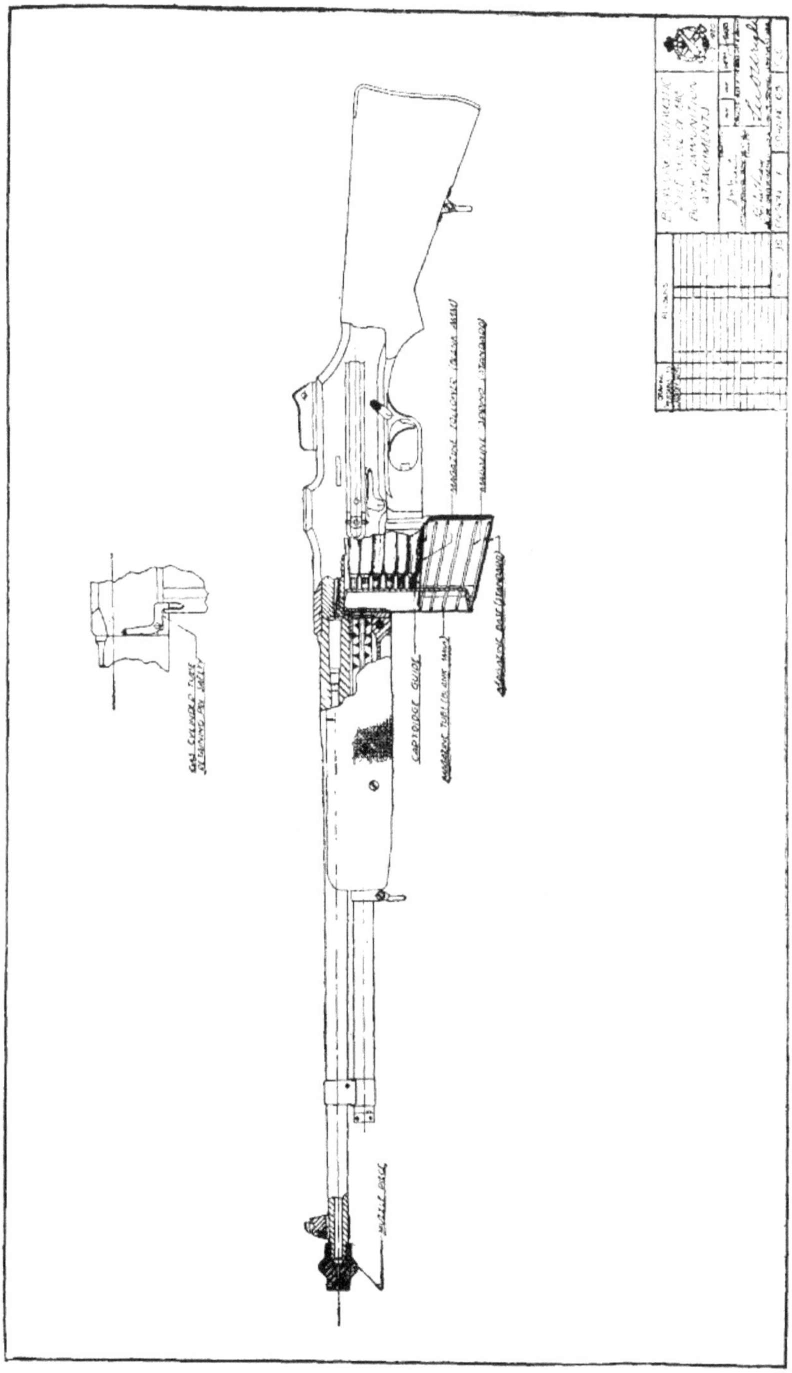